**Steve J. Martin** is an author, business columnist, and director of INFLUENCE AT WORK (UK). His work applying behavioral science to business and public-sector challenges has been featured in broadcast and print media across the world including BBC TV and Radio, MSNBC, the *London Times*, the *New York Times*, the *Los Angeles Times*, *Wired*, and the *Harvard Business Review*. His monthly business columns are read by over 2.5 million readers each month.

An accomplished speaker and consultant, Steve has an extensive global client list. He is a guest lecturer on executive education programs at the London Business School, Cass Business School, and the Judge Business School, University of Cambridge.

He lives in London, UK.

\* \* \*

**Dr. Noah Goldstein** is Associate Professor of Management and Organization, Psychology, and Medicine at UCLA Anderson School of Management. He previously served on the faculty of the University of Chicago Booth School of Business.

Dr. Goldstein has won awards for excellence in both teaching and research.

His research and writing on persuasion and influence have been published in many of the premier business journals. Goldstein's work on persuasion was featured in the *Harvard Business Review* 2009 List of Breakthrough Ideas and has regularly been featured in prominent news outlets such as the *New York Times*, the *Wall Street Journal*, and National Public Radio. In addition to giving keynotes and consulting institutions, Dr. Goldstein has served on the Scientific Advisory Boards of two Fortune Global 500 companies.

He lives in Santa Monica, California.

* * *

**Dr. Robert Cialdini** has spent his entire career researching the science of influence, earning him an international reputation as an expert in the fields of persuasion, compliance, and negotiation. Currently Dr. Cialdini is Regents' Professor Emeritus of Psychology and Marketing at Arizona State University.

As well as his best-selling books, his groundbreaking research has been featured in the most prestigious of scientific journals as well as on TV, radio, and in business and national press throughout the world.

Dr. Cialdini is the president of INFLUENCE AT WORK, a global training, speaking, and certification company. In the field of influence and persuasion he is the *most cited living social psychologist* in the world today.

He lives in Phoenix, Arizona.

# The
# SMALL
# BIG

# The SMALL BIG

---

## SMALL changes
## that spark BIG influence

---

STEVE J. MARTIN,
NOAH J. GOLDSTEIN,
AND ROBERT B. CIALDINI

PROFILE BOOKS

This paperback edition published in 2015

First published in Great Britain in 2014 by
PROFILE BOOKS LTD
3 Holford Yard
Bevin Way
London WC1X 9HD
*www.profilebooks.com*

First published in the United States of America in 2014 by
Business Plus, an imprint of Grand Central Publishing
*www.HatchetteBookGroup.com*

10 9 8 7 6 5 4 3 2 1

Printed and bound in Great Britain by
CPI Group (UK) Ltd, Croydon, CR0 4YY

A CIP catalogue record for this book is available from the British Library.

ISBN 978 1 78125 275 8
eISBN 978 1 78283 075 7

*To Lindsay*

*To Jenessa and my parents, Adelle and Bernie Goldstein*

*To Bobette—the unsung heroine of this book—and to Hailey,
Dawson, and Leia, whom I very much want to like it when they're
old enough to read it*

# Contents

# Introduction

**B**ritney Spears hit the headlines for hers. So did the actors Gérard Depardieu and Lindsay Lohan. But celebrity no-shows aren't just limited to court appearances (or, more accurately, nonappearances). Some celebrities even let down their own fans. The British rock band Oasis earned a reputation for being somewhat less than reliable when it came to show time, and the US country-and-western singer George Jones failed to show up to his concerts on such a regular basis that, for years, he was known to fans as "No-Show Jones."

Unlike these headline grabbers, the no-shows in everyday life don't get much attention. A diner fails to honor a restaurant booking; a citizen misses jury service; a meeting slips the mind of a busy executive; a friend forgets to meet for coffee; or a patient fails to show up for a medical appointment.

Viewed in isolation, these missed appointments don't seem that costly. But every year millions of business meetings, hairdresser appointments, restaurant reservations, sales presentations, and student tutorials are missed. And, when scaled up, these small lapses can have an enormous financial impact.

Take someone who fails to show up for a medical appointment. At first glance it's no big deal. One could easily imagine a busy, overloaded physician viewing a patient no-show as a rare opportunity to catch up on paperwork, make a few calls, or take a short break. But when such incidents become regular occurrences, the cumulative impact of inefficiency, lost income, and sunken costs can be huge. In the United Kingdom no-shows

1

are estimated to cost the National Health Service some £800 million every year; in the United States, some healthcare economists estimate that no-shows create billions of dollars in losses.

In the hospitality industry, when patrons fail to show up for their reservations, restaurants can experience a decline in revenues, dwindling profits, and, if the no-show numbers go uncorrected, even closure.

Other businesses suffer when costly meetings need to be rescheduled because an individual crucial to the decision-making process fails to arrive, or because potential clients who accepted an invitation to a sales presentation, trade show, or convention turn out to be no-shows.

So what can be done?

Fortunately when it comes to persuading people to keep their appointments and, more generally, to live up to their commitments, small changes can have a big impact. In a recent study that we carried out in health centers, we implemented two small changes that resulted in a significant reduction in no-shows. Both changes were costless to implement, but their financial impact could be huge, potentially enabling the healthcare providers concerned to save tens of millions of dollars every year.

We will describe what those two small changes were in one of the chapters that follows (chapter 8 if you can't wait), but it is important to recognize that persuading someone to keep an appointment is just a single example of an influence challenge. There are hundreds of things we need to persuade others to do in lots of different situations and environments.

Regardless of who we need to persuade, what we will consistently reveal throughout this book is a simple truth: *When it comes to influencing the behaviors of others, it is often the smallest changes in approach that make the biggest differences.*

This is a book about how to influence and persuade others in effective and ethical ways. It offers usable information about lots of small but key changes (more than 50 in fact) that you can employ immediately. Importantly, within the chapters that follow, we won't rely on hunches or guesses to identify which particular changes might bring about significantly transformed responses. Instead we will offer evidence based on a large body of persuasion science to show you precisely which small changes can bring about big effects across a wide range of situations.

Over thirty years ago one of us (Robert Cialdini) published *Influence: The Psychology of Persuasion*. That book described the six universal principles of persuasion, identified from a review of the available scientific evidence at the time and from Cialdini's own comprehensive three-year field study. Since then, researchers have confirmed these six principles and practitioners in all sorts of fields continue to put them to use. They are *reciprocity* (people feel obligated to return favors performed for them), *authority* (people look to experts to show them the way), *scarcity* (the less available the resource, the more people want it), *liking* (the more that people like others, the more they want to say yes to them), *consistency* (people want to act consistently with their commitments and values), and *social proof* (people look to what others do in order to guide their own behavior).

In our follow-up book, *Yes! 50 Secrets from the Science of Persuasion*, we offered updated and specific advice about how to employ these principles as well as numerous other strategies informed by persuasion science.

But science rarely stops to take a breath.

Over the last few years, more and more research from fields such as neuroscience, cognitive psychology, social psychology, and behavioral economics has helped to uncover an even greater understanding of how influence, persuasion, and behavior change happens. In this new book, we'll review more than 50 of these new insights and ideas with the majority drawn from research conducted over the last few years.

We have purposely written these insights as short chapters; each should take, on average, no longer than ten minutes or so to read. That will be enough time to allow you to understand the psychological mechanism at play that we, and many other researchers, have confirmed through scientific studies. We'll then quickly move to how you can practically apply the idea or insight across a range of contexts—in business and workplace settings with colleagues, clients, and coworkers; at home with your friends and neighbors; and in a host of other common interactions you may encounter. We will also discuss how to apply these ideas in many common situations, such as face-to-face interactions, group meetings, telephone conversations, email exchanges, and online or social media networks.

In addition to mining insights from the latest persuasion science there is something else new about the material in this book—its focus on the theme of small changes that lead to big effects. For the first time, we'll be considering how to influence and persuade others (in entirely ethical ways) by considering only the smallest changes that are likely to lead to the biggest effects.

We call this type of change a SMALL BIG.

We think that this focus on scientifically informed, small yet high-impact changes is critically important because the approach that people typically use to persuade others is becoming increasingly ineffective.

Most people believe that when making decisions they consider all the available information at their disposal and come to an informed decision about the right course of action. No surprise then, that they believe the same must be true for others, and that the best way to persuade people is to provide them with all the available information and a rationale for why they should pay attention to it.

For example, a medical doctor, on diagnosing one of her patients with a long-term illness which, although not trivial, is eminently treatable, may present that patient with information about what has caused the condition, its etiology, and the prognosis before suggesting a number of steps to manage the condition, such as making dietary changes and taking prescribed medicines at the right time and dosage. An IT director who is becoming increasingly frustrated by the growing number of employees downloading unauthorized software onto company computers might send out a communication to his employees describing, at length, the potential implications of their actions and the reasons why they are considered infringements of company policy.

It's not just physicians and IT directors who attempt to inform people into a desirable change. We all do it. Want to persuade that new client that your product is more effective than your competitors' and therefore warrants that 20 percent price premium? Then provide a body of additional information and rebuttals that support your claims. Want to convince your team that your latest change program is different from the dozen or so you have rolled out in the past? Then provide lots of reasons and show them how everyone will benefit this time around. Want to persuade your clients to sign up to your company's stock market investment plan? Then carefully walk them through a highly technical analysis of your company's investment history, ensuring that you highlight the most impressive results. Want to get your kids to do their homework and go to bed on time? Then tell them about studies showing how doing homework increases their chances of getting into an Ivy League school, and maybe follow up with some research results on the beneficial effects of sleep.

Yet the latest persuasion science research reveals an often overlooked insight that goes a long way to explaining why strategies that simply attempt to inform people into making a change carry a high likelihood of failure.

5

In short, it is not information per se that leads people to make decisions, but the context in which that information is presented. We are living in the single most information-overloaded, stimulation-saturated environment that has ever existed. People just don't have the capacity to fully consider every piece of information in their time-scarce, attention-challenged, busy lives. Successful influence is increasingly governed by context rather than cognition and by the psychological environment in which such information is presented. As a result, anyone can significantly increase their ability to influence and persuade others by not only attempting to inform or educate people into change, but also by simply making small shifts in their approach to link their message to deeply felt human motivations. A small change in the setting, framing, timing, or context of *how information is conveyed* can dramatically alter *how it is received and acted upon*.

As behavioral scientists who study both the theory and practice of influence and persuasion, we are constantly fascinated by not only how breathtakingly slight the changes to a communicator's message can be that spawn enormous effects, but also how rarely those changes require large investments in time, effort, or money. Throughout this book we will be careful to pinpoint which small changes to make and how to employ them strategically and ethically so that you can produce BIG differences in your ability to influence others without resorting to costly financial levers (incentives, discounts, rebates, penalties, etc.) or using up valuable time and resources.

We will also point to a number of mysteries and pose a series of questions that can be explained by a better understanding of persuasion science. For example:

- What small alteration can you make to an email that could make your business partners easier to negotiate with?

- What can hurricanes, 99-cent price endings, and frozen yogurt teach you about small changes that can lead to effective persuasion?
- What small changes in approach can help you to host more productive meetings?
- And what small, costless shift in language can motivate others (and yourself for that matter) to complete a goal such as achieving a sales target, losing weight, taking up a new hobby, or getting your kids to complete their homework?

It is perhaps easy, in today's fast-paced, data-rich world, where information updates are immediately available at the click of a button or the swipe of a screen, to dismiss the importance of small changes in the context of that information. But to do so would be a mistake.

While there can be no doubt that new technologies and instantly accessible information have brought us wonderful benefits, the cognitive hardware that we use to process that information has remained largely unchanged for centuries. Ironically, as the amount of information we have at our disposal to make better decisions increases, the less likely we are to use all of that information when we do have to decide. People today are just as likely to be influenced by small changes in communication context as were our ancestors from hundreds or thousands of years ago.

When it comes to influencing and persuading others in ethical and effective ways, *small is very much the new big*. As you will begin to see in the pages ahead, by simply incorporating small, scientifically informed changes into a persuasive appeal, the impact can be great.

So let's begin our journey into this new science of persuasion by showing how small changes in the wording of a letter persuaded thousands of citizens to take action and pay the taxes they owed, earning the relevant government office hundreds of millions of pounds in additional revenues. Then, let's consider the implications for your own persuasive efforts.

Steve J. Martin
Noah J. Goldstein
Robert B. Cialdini

# CHAPTER 1

## What SMALL BIG can persuade people to pay their taxes on time?

Like tax collectors in a lot of countries, officials in Britain's Her Majesty's Revenue & Customs (HMRC) had a problem: Too many citizens weren't submitting their tax returns and paying what they owed on time.

For many years officials at HMRC had created a variety of letters and communications targeted at late-payers. The majority of these approaches focused on the various consequences that late-payers would face if they failed to respond and pay on time: interest charges, late fees, and legal action. For some folks these traditional approaches worked well, but for many others they did not. So in early 2009, in consultation with our company INFLUENCE AT WORK, HMRC decided to try an alternative approach informed by persuasion science. All it involved was one small change: a single sentence added to their standard letter.

This small change was remarkable not only for its simplicity, but also for the huge difference it made in response rates. The new letters led to the collection of £560 million of the £650 million debt that was the focus of the pilot studies, representing a clearance rate of 86 percent. To put this into perspective, the previous year HMRC had collected £290 million of a possible £510 million—a clearance rate of just 57 percent.

Overall, the new letters, combined with other best practices informed from the private collections industry, contributed to the collection of £5.6 billion more overdue revenue than had been collected the previous year. Additionally HMRC reduced the amount of debt on its books by £3.5 billion. Considering how small and cost-effective the actual changes were, the overall impact is nothing short of astonishing.

So what exactly was this small change to the letter? We simply (and truthfully) informed the recipients of the large number of citizens who actually do pay their taxes on time.

But why would so many thousands of people feel compelled to mail in their checks on the basis of such a small change to a standard letter? The answer lies in a fundamental principle of human behavior that scientists call *social proof*—the evidence of the crowd. It means that people's behavior is largely shaped by the behaviors of others around them, especially those with whom they strongly identify.

Researchers have been studying the phenomenon for decades, and it's not only humans that are influenced by its immense power. Birds flock. Cattle herd. Fish school. Social insects swarm. So fundamental is the draw of what others are doing that even organisms without a brain cortex are subject to its force. The concept of social proof may not be new, but we are learning more about its impact and how best to employ it all the time.

That a context of consensus will frequently trump effortful cognition could be seen both as worrying as well as comforting to people. We worry about being seen as lemming-like, of submitting total control over our decisions to the crowd. Yet we can also take comfort because such conformity mostly leads us to the right decisions.

Following the crowd is not an action that is simply fueled by a need to keep up with the Joneses. It is more fundamental than that, striking at the heart of three simple, yet powerful, under-lying human motivations: the motivation to make accurate decisions as efficiently as possible, the motivation to affiliate with and to gain the approval of others, and the motivation to see oneself in a positive light.

The seemingly small change made to the UK tax letters led to such huge differences because it was able to pull on each of these three motivations at the same time. In the context of a busy, overloaded life, "doing what most others are doing" can be a remarkably efficient shortcut to a good decision, regardless of whether that decision concerns which movie to watch, which restaurant to frequent, or, in the case of the UK's HMRC, whether or when to pay your taxes.

Drawing attention to the fact that most people do pay taxes on time aligns to a desire to affiliate with others. After all, by following what most people are already doing, there's a good chance that we'll gain their approval and increase the odds of making social connections. Finally, in the particular case of the British citizens receiving the HMRC letter, the third motiva-tion, a desire to see oneself in a positive light, was active too. Most people probably don't take pride in being a deadbeat. It's certainly easier to be a leech on society if one believes that everyone else is a leech, too. But in learning that so many British citizens do pay their taxes on time, those few who don't will feel more like freeloaders. In the face of that information, following the majority by paying one's taxes helped restore one's self-image as an individual who does their fair share.

Given how powerful the concept of social proof can be, it is surprising how largely dismissive people are about its powerful effect on them. In one set of studies that two of us conducted with behavioral scientists Jessica Nolan, Wes Schulz, and Vladas Griskevicius, we asked several hundred homeowners in California to report on the extent to which they believed four

11

different potential reasons for conserving energy actually influenced their decisions to try to reduce their overall home energy consumption. The four potential reasons were (1) conserving energy helps the environment; (2) conserving energy protects future generations; (3) conserving energy saves them money; (4) many of their neighbors are already conserving energy.

The homeowners resoundingly rated conserving energy because "many of their neighbors are already" doing so as having the least influence on their own behavior. Armed with this information, we then conducted an experiment in a southern California neighborhood, randomly assigning homes to display one of four signs on their front doors, each employing one of the four reasons listed above. Some residents were reminded of how much conserving saves the environment, others how conserving protects future generations, and yet others how much money they could save by conserving. Finally, a fourth group of residents was informed of findings from a recent survey indicating that the majority of their neighbors were actively trying to conserve energy.

When we measured their energy usage nearly a month later, we discovered that the social proof communication was the single *most* effective message when it came to actually changing their behavior— even though a majority of respondents in the earlier study had rejected it as having any sway. Interestingly, the majority of people in the earlier study thought that the most influential reason to conserve energy was that it protects the environment. But, in fact, in the second study, that environmental message hardly affected energy usage at all.

The truth is, not only are people pretty poor at recognizing what will influence their future behavior, it turns out that they are also not that well attuned to what persuaded them after the event either. As part of a TV news magazine program one of us was asked to assist with a segment of the show that sought to identify the reasons why people might be persuaded to help others in a series of everyday (nonemergency) settings. At a busy New York City subway station we hired researchers to count the number of commuters who donated to a street musician as they walked past.

After a short time a small change was made to the situation that had an immediate and impressive impact. Just before an approaching (and unsuspecting) commuter reached the musician, another person (who was in on the act) would drop a few coins into the musician's hat in view of the approaching commuter. The result? An eight-fold increase in the number of commuters who chose to make a donation.

In a series of post-study interviews with commuters who did donate, every one of them failed to attribute their action to the fact that they had just seen someone else give money first. Instead they provided alternative justifications: "I liked the song he was playing"; "I'm a generous person"; and "I felt sorry for the guy."

That people are generally poor at recognizing the factors that influence their behaviors both before *and after* an event raises an immediate implication for any business or organization that invests time, effort, and often considerable dollars asking their customers and clients what actually drives their buying decisions and behaviors. Although we are confident that many customers will happily provide answers, we are less confident that the answers they provide will be an accurate reflection of what happens in reality, resulting in marketing strategies based on those answers having high failure rates.

So rather than basing your influence strategies on what people say will influence their decisions, one small change that you can make immediately is to simply and honestly depict what the majority of others who are similar to your target audience are already doing that you would like your audience to do, too.

For example, a business development executive seeking to attract customers to a presentation about a new product could increase attendance by first inviting those who will be most likely to attend. Then the executive could honestly point out to his next group of targets that "many other people have already accepted our invitation to attend." This small shift can be very effective even if those targets have previously stated that attendance by others will have no influence over their own decisions to attend.

Social proof appeals can be further enhanced by applying one other insight gleaned from the UK tax letter studies—adding extra specificity. Some letters highlighted not just the number of people nationally who paid their taxes on time but also the percentage of people who lived in the same zip code as the letter recipient. This approach yielded a response rate of 79 percent, compared to a typical response rate of 67 percent to the standard letters.

Of course it's not just governments and tax officials who can benefit from the application of these insights. Most businesses and organizations, from global powerhouses to local housing associations, have a need to collect funds from customers and clients in a timely fashion. Where evidence exists that the majority of customers and clients do pay on time, our recommendation is to present such salient information on invoices and statements. Although it is unlikely that this small change alone will influence everyone to pay on time, it should certainly improve payment rates, freeing up organizational resources to target the minority who actively avoid paying on time or even evade making payments entirely.

Notice too the importance of focusing your audiences' attention on behaviors that are both frequently adopted *and* desirable. In a study that one of us led with physicians Suraj Bassi and Rupert Dunbar-Rees, we found that health centers that prominently published the number of people who failed to attend a health appointment the previous month typically saw an *increase* in no-shows the following month. As we mentioned in our introduction, the cost of no-shows can lead to huge losses and inefficiencies, not just in health centers, but in all types of business and public sector settings. So a small and costless change such as focusing on desirable behaviors can make an extraordinary difference.

Of course, a strategy of highlighting how many people are carrying out desirable behaviors such as paying taxes, keeping appointments, or doing homework assignments on time won't be so successful if the behavior or change you are trying to effect isn't already practiced by a majority of people. In such cases, as tempting as it might be to simply invent a majority, we would strongly urge against such an idea. Not only would this be unethical, but should it be discovered that your social proof appeal was manufactured, any future influence attempts you make will, at best, struggle for credibility and, at worst, simply become toxic.

However, there are alternatives; in fact, two specific approaches can be quite effective. The first is to highlight behaviors that are largely approved of in a given situation. Behavioral scientists label what most others approve/disapprove in a situation the *injunctive* norm. For example, highlighting survey results that have found that a majority of people support a particular cause can play an important role in helping to shape future change: 80 percent of Californian residents believe it is important that they play their part in energy-saving programs, and nine out of ten employees said they would be interested in learning more about how to lead a healthier lifestyle. In such instances the small BIG would be for a communicator to make such injunctive norms part of their message strategy.

It can also be effective to publish absolute numbers that suggest the widespread adoption of an idea or behavior.

Opower is an Arlington, Virginia–based company that provides energy reports that encourage homeowners to save energy. On its website Opower honestly publicizes that its programs have helped people save "over 6 billion kilowatt hours of electricity" and "over $750 million on energy bills," messages that can be pretty effective at spurring people to take part, even without specific evidence that the majority of people like them has already joined in. Messages that point to *growing* numbers of people can also be a useful strategy, particularly in the early stages of campaigns when you are seeking to gain momentum. For example, a blogger whose web traffic over the past few months has risen from a couple of hundred visits a week to close to a thousand might highlight the five-fold increase in such a short space of time. A Facebook user might promote the increasing number of "likes" they have gained.

Of course it would be naive for us to claim that social proof strategies such as the one we describe in the UK tax letter campaign provide an answer to every situation in which we want to change a set of behaviors. But given that some of the latest social-proof strategies are now generating *billions* rather than millions or thousands in extra revenues and efficiencies, it certainly seems to make sense to have an understanding of their uses.

Which leads us to a related question: Under what circumstances might people go out of their way to actually avoid following what others around them are doing?

## CHAPTER 2

# What SMALL BIG can persuade people to go against the crowd?

Whether it's choosing the busy restaurant over the quieter one, being swept along by the momentum of a wave* at a sporting event, or, as detailed in the previous chapter, persuading people to pay their taxes on time, social proof can be a hugely efficient decision shortcut, serving to help us not only make mostly accurate decisions but also form bonds and connections to others. Such is the draw of wanting to follow the behavior of others that going against the pull of the crowd is not only emotionally distressing but, according to recent neuroscience research, it can even be painful.

In a modern-day replication of Solomon Asch's classic conformity studies from the 1950s, a team led by neuroscientist Gregory Berns told a group of people that, as part of a study on perception, they would be shown a series of 3-D objects and

---

*Amazingly researchers have studied the concept of the so-called Mexican wave at sports arenas and find that they share some remarkable consistencies regardless of the sport being played or the cultural origin of the crowd. For example researchers at Eötvös University in Budapest, Hungary, have identified that most waves move in a clockwise direction, are typically around 15 seats in width, and travel at a steady speed of 12 meters (40 feet) per second. As for how many people are required to start a wave? According to the same researchers, less than three dozen.

would later be asked to identify which objects were the same in terms of size and shape and which were different. The researchers also pointed out that while everyone would be involved in the study, only one member of the group would be hooked up to the functional magnetic resonance imaging (fMRI) brain scanner in the next room and that everyone should remain in the waiting room while they set up the machine. However, all this was just an elaborate ploy, because everyone in the group was part of the study and in on the act. Everyone, that is, except for the person hooked up to the MRI—the genuine study participant—who was about to become the subject of a fascinating experiment designed to identify what happens in our brains when we go against the group consensus.

Having been "selected," the study participant was then connected to the scanner, shown a series of pairs of 3-D images, and asked which were the same and which were different. However, before answering, the participant was first informed that the "volunteers" in the other room had also been shown the images and for each pair of images had made a decision about what the correct answer was. Sometimes the group gave a deliberately wrong answer in order to see whether the person would cave to the social pressure. Despite the fact that most "selected" participants knew the group's wrong answers didn't seem right, they still conformed to them about 40 percent of the time.

Perhaps more interesting, though, was the finding that when the study participant made an independent judgment that went against the consensus of the group, the areas of the brain associated with emotion were activated, suggesting that there is a real emotional cost to going against the group and the price we pay is a painful one.

It can be especially hard to go against those groups that we consider to be particularly important to our own social identity—in other words, groups that help us define who we are and how we see ourselves. For example, recall in the previous chapter how officials from the UK tax office were able to increase the number of people persuaded to pay their taxes on time simply by pointing out prominently on reminder letters that most people already do pay on time. Remember also that when extra specificity was added to the letters, informing recipients that the majority of people living in the same zip code had paid on time, response rates rose to 79 percent compared to a standard response rate of 67 percent.

A third letter was also used, one that tugged much harder on each individual's social identity. Instead of pointing out that the majority of people who lived in the same zip code had submitted their taxes on time, these letters included the name of the town. This small change led to an even bigger increase in response rates, with almost 83 percent of people taking action.

These results show that one small BIG that communicators can employ is to ensure that their message aligns closely with the social identity of their target group. For example, the online world provides a piece of data that can be leveraged for greater persuasiveness in this way: IP addresses. Organizations could use IP addresses, which provide the location of visitors to their websites, to convey the social proof of people from a specific area. In other words, rather than conveying the same, less specific social proof information to website visitors from New York City and Houston ("81 percent of people choose the premium package!"), the site could be programmed to provide even more tailored social identity information ("82 percent of New Yorkers choose the premium package!" and "80 percent of Houstonites choose the premium package!"), assuming of course those numbers were true.

The highlighting of more similar social proof information doesn't just extend to locational similarities. It can work for people's names too—a concept we refer to as *nominative* similarities. During the 2012 US presidential election one notable email appeal from the Obama for America campaign invited registered voters to see how many other people who shared the same name as them had voted early. For example, one read, "Hey Emily, this is cool. You can see exactly how many other people called Emily have already voted."

Having taken a look, users were then invited to send the link to their friends. "Now share it with some people you know—like Megan, Tom, Carrie, Abby, Mo and Danny so they can see how many people with their names voted too."

But just as people are often motivated to match the common behaviors of the groups to which they belong or want to belong, they are also motivated to avoid the common behaviors of those groups to which they don't want to belong. In one fascinating examination of this idea, Jonah Berger, researcher and author of the bestselling book *Contagious*, together with Chip Heath, the bestselling co-author of *Switch* and *Made to Stick*, examined how students in one college dormitory who had recently purchased a charity wristband would react to seeing that students in a comparatively "geeky" dormitory had adopted the practice of wearing the same wristband. To answer this question, they first had research assistants go door-to-door in the "target dorm" (i.e., the nongeeky one) offering the wristbands to students in exchange for making a donation of any amount to a certain charity. A week later, these research assistants did the same thing at a nearby "academic dorm"—one that had a reputation for being geeky because these students engaged in additional academic activities, such as taking extra courses and leading group discussions. The researchers knew that those in the target dorm would see those in the geeky dorm wearing the wristbands because the two dorms ate at the same dining hall.

It's important to note that, at the same time research assistants were offering wristbands to the target dorm, they were also offering wristbands to a control dorm on the other side of campus. Although target dorm students were expected to interact with the students from the geeky dorm, neither set of students was expected to interact much with the control dorm students due to the distance between them.

The results were most revealing. The researchers found that following the purchase of the wristbands by the geeky dorm, there was a 32 percent decrease in the number of target dorm students who wore the wristband. How did the researchers know that this huge abandonment of the wristband was primarily due to these students wanting to avoid associating themselves with the geeky dorm, rather than simply becoming bored wearing the wristband? It turns out that there was only a 6 percent decrease in the number of control dorm students (the ones who didn't interact with the geeky dorm students) who wore the wristband over the same time period.

Berger and Heath suggest that the motivation to disassociate oneself from groups is strongest when the behavior in question is openly public to other people. To test this idea, the researchers conducted another experiment, this time in the domain of food choice. They told some undergraduate participants that the biggest consumers of junk food on campus were undergraduates; others were told it was graduate students (a group with which undergrads typically don't want to associate). The researchers then had the participants choose products to eat (some healthy and others junk food), either in public view of other participants or in private. Berger and Heath found that when the participants chose privately, there was no difference in the number that chose junk food between those told that undergrads were the biggest consumers of junk food on campus and those told that it was grad students. However, when their behavior was made public to other undergraduates, the participants were far less likely to choose junk food when they were told that grad students were the biggest junk food consumers.

Taken together, this research suggests that companies looking to gain new market segments need to be careful to avoid situations in which adoption of the product by the new segment might cause its current users to abandon it in order to disassociate themselves from the new adopters. More generally, this research suggests that anyone looking to discourage certain behaviors—be it unhealthy eating, littering, or showing up late for work—should consider pairing those behaviors with an undesirable identity.

We are reminded of a recent television commercial that Samsung put out against its arch nemesis, Apple. It features a number of teenage Apple users waiting in line for the next iPhone. One person in line reveals that he recently bought a Samsung phone and that the only reason he's on line is that he's saving a spot for a couple of other people. A little later we learn the identities of the people for whom he was saving a spot. It turns out to be the people that teenagers definitely want to dissociate themselves from the most: their middle-aged parents!

## CHAPTER 3

# What SMALL change to the way you frame a message can lead to BIG differences in outcome?

In the previous chapters we described how the effectiveness of your proposition or request can be significantly improved by making a small shift in your message that signals to your audience that similar others are already behaving in desirable ways. We also provided evidence that if those people also share a social identity with your audience and belong to the same in-group, then your message will likely be more persuasive still. But there is another important consideration—one that might lead you to make another small change to your approach that could lead to a big effect. It concerns the framing of your message to reveal how common, or uncommon, the behavior you're advocating is. Let's take an example.

Imagine for a few minutes that a friend has the nasty habit of never covering his nose or mouth when he sneezes. Should you highlight the positive aspects of those who cover their faces when they sneeze, or would you be more effective if you instead emphasized the negative aspects of those who don't?

Psychologist Hart Blanton and his colleagues believed that the successful framing of your message will depend on your friend's perceptions of the relevant social norms. As we mentioned earlier, people are motivated to conform to social norms. Yet, people often seek to define themselves based on what makes them unique. This means that in situations in which they are led to think about the implications of their behavior for their identity, they are typically more attentive to the costs and benefits of deviating from, rather than conforming to, the perceived norm. Thus, attempts to influence other people's actions should be more successful when messages are framed in terms of *deviating* from the perceived social norm rather than *conforming* to it.

For example, if your friend believes covering one's face while sneezing is the norm, then a message framed to accentuate the negative characteristics of those who deviate from the perceived norm should be most effective (e.g., "Those who *don't* cover their face when sneezing are very irresponsible"). However if he believes that not covering one's face while sneezing is the norm, then a message framed to accentuate the positive characteristics of those who deviate from the perceived norm might work better (e.g., "Those who *do* cover their face are very responsible").

In an experiment designed to test this hypothesis, Blanton and his colleagues asked study participants to read one of two newspaper articles in which the majority of students opting for flu shots was varied: One article claimed that most students were getting the shot, whereas the other claimed that the majority of students were *not* getting the shot. Next, the participants read a second article characterizing the behavior of those who do and don't get flu shots. The message from this second article was framed one of two ways: Either the decision to get immunized was linked with positive characteristics (e.g., "Those who *do* get immunized are considerate of others") or the decision not to get immunized was linked with negative characteristics (e.g., "Those who *don't* get immunized are inconsiderate of others").

Consistent with the researchers' expectations, participants in the study were more influenced by the message that described the characteristics of people who deviated from, rather than conformed to, the norm: In other words, when participants thought most other students were getting flu shots, they were more persuaded by the message characterizing those who did *not* get flu shots, and when they thought most other students were *not* getting flu shots, they were more persuaded by the message characterizing those who *did* get flu shots.

This study provides a neat demonstration of how, by first informing people about the social norms of a behavior in question, your subsequent message can be improved by describing the characteristics of those who might deviate from it. A health club, keen to maintain high standards of cleanliness in its changing rooms, might point out to new members that most other members place their towels in the laundry baskets rather than leave them on the floor, and the few members who do not are being disrespectful to others. Recently hired employees might be informed during their orientation program that most of their colleagues accurately and honestly complete their expenses by the due date, and those who don't are letting down their department. A newly diagnosed diabetic could be informed that most patients like them quickly get into the habit of checking their blood sugars before they drive, and the few who don't could be putting other drivers at risk.

But wait a minute. With the gym member, new employee, and diabetic patient examples, as well as the flu shot study, the people being informed of the social norm of the situation really aren't already aware of the norm. The question is, would a similar approach work for those individuals who have preexisting beliefs about how common or uncommon certain behaviors already are? It turns out that it can.

In a separate experiment that Blanton conducted with Regina Van den Eijnden and other researchers, study participants were first asked to report on their perceptions of certain healthy practices on their university campus. Two weeks later, they read a set of phony testimonials from other students that either ascribed positive traits (e.g., mature, smart) to those who do engage in healthy behaviors, or negative traits (e.g., immature, stupid) to those who don't. The researchers found that the more common the participants perceived healthy practices to be, the more they were influenced by the message that negatively depicted those who do *not* have healthy habits. In contrast, the less common that the participants perceived healthy behaviors to be, the more they were influenced by the message that positively portrayed those who *do* have healthy habits.

This and other similar findings on the topic point to a small but important task that a communicator needs to undertake before deciding how to frame a persuasive message: Consider the audience's perceptions of social norms before characterizing the behaviors that deviate from that norm.

Accordingly, when seeking to improve timekeeping and efficiencies in her office, an executive would be advised to consider her workers' perceptions of how much of a problem it is when meetings start late. If the perception is that it's a problem that occurs too often, then her message should focus on depicting the positive traits of those employees who do arrive in a timely fashion. However, if the common belief is that lateness isn't too much of an issue, then her message should instead focus on the negative traits of latecomers.

More generally we hope that through the proper implementation of small and scientifically informed persuasion attempts, we can have a world in which people are healthier, coworkers are more compliant with your requests, and salad bar sneeze guards become totally unnecessary.

# CHAPTER 4

## What SMALL BIG can help to right a wrong?

Back in the 1990s, New York mayor Rudy Giuliani and other government officials around the United States embraced an idea that was proposed by social scientists James Wilson and George Kelling known as the "broken windows theory." This theory suggested that even small signs of disorder—such as a single broken window in a housing project or a storefront that goes unfixed—could encourage more widespread negative behavior because of the social norms that it communicates.

Giuliani, his police chief, and other government officials who subscribed to this theory focused their attention on combating small but powerful signs of disorder and petty crime. Their efforts included removing graffiti, sweeping streets, and enacting a zero-tolerance policy for seemingly minor violations like subway fare evasion. These efforts have been linked by politicians to the reduction in other more serious crimes and violations, although the scientific evidence on this point has remained inconclusive. However, research by behavioral scientists Kees Keizer, Siegwart Lindenberg, and Linda Steg seems to provide solid evidence regarding the influence of such seemingly small norm violations on other behaviors in the environment. Even more importantly, their research points to small changes that can lead to big improvements for policy makers and businesses alike.

In their field experiments Keizer and his colleagues tested to what extent various subtle signs of disorder in an environment could influence the proliferation of other undesirable behaviors. In one study the researchers found the perfect setting for their test: an alleyway near a Dutch shopping mall where shoppers typically parked their bikes. While the shoppers were at the mall, the researchers affixed one of the store's advertisements on the handlebar of each bicycle with an elastic band. In one condition, the researchers left the alleyway just as they found it; in a second condition, they added graffiti to the alleyway. Because there were no garbage bins in the area, shoppers returning from the mall to find a printed advertisement attached to the handlebars of their bicycle had a simple choice. Do they remove the advertisement and take it home with them—or do they instead drop it on the ground?

The results revealed that 33 percent of the bicycle owners littered the paper when there was no graffiti to be seen in the alleyway. However, 69 percent did so when graffiti was present.

In another of their fascinating field experiments, Keizer and his colleagues went to a parking lot that had multiple pedestrian entrances and blocked off one of those entrances with a series of temporary fences. Signage on the fencing indicated that people returning to their cars should not use that entrance but instead should enter the lot through the other entrance, located approximately 200 yards away. However, the researchers left just enough of a gap in the fencing that a person could pass through if he or she really wanted. They also placed a sign on the fencing that told people that locking their bicycles to the fencing was prohibited. The only aspect of the study that Keizer and his colleagues varied was whether four bicycles were simply parked next to the fencing or were instead all locked to it.

The outcome? When the bicycles were simply positioned next to the fence, 27 percent of the pedestrians stepped through the gap in the fence in direct violation of the signage. However, when the four bikes were locked to the fence in violation of the other signage, a whopping 82 percent of the pedestrians stepped through the gap.

The research we're describing to this point demonstrates that when people observe that their peers have violated one social norm, not only are they potentially more likely to violate that same norm themselves—but they are also more likely to violate a related but different social norm. For example, a dog walker might allow his dog to foul a park not because he observes another dog owner allowing her dog to do so, but because he sees other signs of social disorder in the park, such as litter or people dropping cigarette butts. Workers in an office, walking past the photocopier and paper shredder area and noticing that it is untidy and strewn with scrap paper, might subsequently be more likely to contravene other office norms by leaving their dirty coffee cups on the counter or failing to wipe up spillages in the kitchen area.

But could observing a seemingly small violation in an environment actually cause people to steal when they otherwise wouldn't have? To address this question, the researchers placed a stamped and addressed envelope clearly containing some money halfway in a mailbox so that it was visible and accessible to passersby. The only aspect of the study that Keizer altered was whether there was litter on the ground surrounding the mailbox. When there was no litter in sight, only 13 percent of passersby stole the envelope and the money inside it. However, when the environment was littered, the theft rate nearly doubled—approximately 25 percent stole the envelope!

These findings show just how powerful subtle cues in a surrounding environment can be in terms of influencing people's behavior. As a result, anyone who has a responsibility or interest in encouraging pro-social and desirable behaviors should consider not just the small changes that can be made to their message, but also the small changes that can be made to the environment, recognizing that frequently it is both easier and more efficient to change people's environments than their minds.

Furthermore, this work suggests that allowing visible signs of norm violations that seem relatively unimportant might elicit norm violations in much more important areas. For example, retail outlets might think that occasional litter in the dressing rooms or bathrooms is not worth worrying about; however, this persuasive research suggests that litter might actually increase theft from the store. At work, allowing certain aspects of the office to remain disorderly or in disrepair could trickle down to subtly influence the workforce to slack off or, even worse, engage in some sort of workplace malfeasance.

So what small BIGs could managers, city council members, or even policy makers undertake that could lead to big differences in encouraging and maintaining desirable behaviors in their communities and public places?

One potential small change comes from a relatively new insight gleaned from recent social psychological research conducted by the researchers of the studies we described above. Contrary to common belief, arranging for people to inhabit an ordered environment (no dirty cups in the staff kitchen, a litter-free park, gleaming sidewalks) does not create the strongest context for encouraging desirable behaviors. Instead the strongest context for encouraging desirable behaviors comes from evidence that clearly conveys other people's respect for norms. Therefore the most effective small BIG is not to arrange for people to inhabit an already ordered environment, but instead for people to inhabit an environment where they can witness order being restored. In other words, in an office environment, the best small BIG action might be to change the times when kitchen and staff changing room areas are cleaned. Rather than have cleaners at the ready after everyone has left for the day, it might be better to arrange some overlap so that staffs can see the restoration of their environment.

A related small BIG that government officials could undertake would be to develop programs that encourage citizens not simply to refrain from undesirable actions, but to undo the undesirable actions of others in a public way. Municipalities could allocate resources for the formation and/or support of citizens groups who want to demonstrate their disapproval of disordered environments by cleaning debris from lakes and beaches, graffiti from buildings, and litter from streets. A study by one of us, with Raymond Reno and Carl Kallgren, suggests that the overall effect could be dramatic. It showed that, under normal circumstances, passersby given handbills littered 38 percent of the time. But, passersby who first saw a man *pick up* someone else's litter from the environment littered the handbill only 4 percent of the time.

It would be a stretch, of course, to claim that a failure to police a person's habit of leaving decaying fish tacos or four-week-old milk in the company fridge will lead to your company becoming the next Enron. But we will claim that because contexts can shape behavior as much as any amount of informational content, even seemingly small changes to an environment can make a big difference.

## CHAPTER 5

# How could a SMALL change in name make a BIG difference to your game?

In late October 2012 Hurricane Sandy bulldozed its way through the Caribbean and across the mid-Atlantic before hitting land again in the northeastern United States and leaving a trail of destruction and devastation in its wake. Violent gusts nearing 100 mph accompanied by lashing rain left widespread damage estimated at over $75 billion. In the aftermath, many thousands of individuals as well as organizations such as the American Red Cross and the United Nations marshaled and directed resources toward cleanup and relief operations. Corporations and businesses helped, too, as did a number of network news channels that held telethons and made appeals that generated millions of dollars in donations.

The role played by the news networks wasn't just limited to encouraging contributions that supported relief efforts. They were also responsible for generating a series of unofficial names for the hurricane—from provocative to downright fear-inducing. "Snowicane" was one such example presumably designed to highlight the avalanche proportions of projected snowfall that would accompany Sandy. "Frankenstorm" was another—a reference to the storm's close proximity to Halloween.

While we are not aware of evidence that suggests assigning a hurricane an unofficial fear-inducing name leads to an increase in donations after the event, there is evidence that the *official* name given to a hurricane can have a surprising influence on whether certain individuals will donate. Not only is this evidence surprising, it can also offer some important insight into how a small change you can make to your messages can make a big difference when it comes to persuading others.

Psychology professor Jesse Chandler highlighted an intriguing finding from an analysis of donations made in response to fundraising appeals after devastating hurricanes. Curiously, people were more likely to donate if the initial of their first name matched the name given to the hurricane. Chandler found, for example, that people whose names began with the letter R, such as Robert or Rosemary, were 260 percent more likely to donate to the Hurricane Rita relief appeal than people whose names didn't begin with the letter R. He found a similar effect after Hurricane Katrina, with folks whose names started with a K significantly more motivated to donate funds to help relieve the devastation and displacement caused. In every case going back many years, a similar pattern emerged, with disproportionate numbers of donations coming from those with the same initial as the hurricane.

In his book *Drunk Tank Pink*, marketing professor Adam Alter makes a noteworthy point. If people *are* more likely to donate to hurricane relief programs that share their initials, then the entity responsible for assigning hurricane names, the World Meteorological Organization, has the power to increase charitable giving simply by giving hurricanes more commonly occurring names. Given the advances in meteorological forecasting in recent years, it should be possible to identify the areas where storms will hit, take a look at the voting register for those areas, and then choose a name for the hurricane that closely matches frequently occurring names in that area.

At first glance, insights such as these seem like idle curiosities researched by wacky scientists in an attempt to provide an eyebrow-raising headline or an inane topic of conversation for next weekend's dinner party. But to dismiss these findings as inconsequential would dismiss a fundamental and powerful feature of human psychology. The truth is, our names matter to us.

You can probably recall a time when you have found yourself deep in conversation with a colleague or a friend, perhaps at a conference, in a business meeting, or at a party. The kind of conversation that captured your complete attention. In fact you were so focused on what was being said that you were oblivious to all the other activities and conversations going on around you. But then you heard your name mentioned from another part of the room and instantly your attention was diverted. It's almost as if you possessed an invisible antenna that was constantly scanning the environment, ready and waiting to tune in to any mentions of your name. Such is the prevalence of this phenomenon that psychologists even have a name for it: "The Cocktail Party Phenomenon."

Should you need further convincing of how important people's names are to them, then you might like to try this little experiment next time you're in a meeting or with a group of friends. Hand out a blank piece of paper to everyone in the room and simply ask them to write down their five favorite letters of the alphabet. If they are anything like the subjects in the studies where this has been done, when you review their choices you will likely notice an uncanny similarity between the letters they have chosen and their own names, especially their initials.

So how can insights such as these help you to successfully influence others?

Given that a necessary part of any persuasion strategy is to get someone's attention, it seems logical to explicitly use someone's name more often when seeking to influence them or, at the very least, signal that your request or message has some connection to their name. For example, an experiment we conducted in partnership with a team of British physicians found that simply including a patient's first name in an SMS (short message service) text reminding them to attend a health appointment led to a 57 percent reduction in no-shows compared to reminders that didn't include their first name. Interestingly, including a patient's full name (e.g., John Smith) or a more formal salutation (e.g., Mr. Smith) made no difference at all. *It was only when a patient's first name was used that it had an effect.*

small BIGs like these aren't just being deployed in an effort to reduce inefficiencies such as those produced by people failing to show up to their doctor's appointments. They are also being used to persuade people to pay fines that they owe. One study conducted by the Behavioural Insights Team, a crack squad of behavioral scientists, originally working at the heart of the British government but now a commerical body, found that sending a text message requesting payment of a fine that included an offender's first name along with the amount owed increased response rates by almost half—from 23 percent to 33 percent—compared to the same message that didn't include the offender's name.

The attention-grabbing nature of a name could also prove fruitful for those charged with generating support for new business initiatives and work programs. When it comes to naming that new project, you may be tempted to consider an ambiguous, mysterious-sounding name in the hope that it will spark interest, get people's attention, and mobilize them behind your efforts. The hurricane studies, however, suggest an alternative approach. Rather than attempting to evoke the passions and emotions of your employees by likening your initiative to some kind of mythological bird that is reborn from its own ashes, you might receive more support if you simply look down the list of people who work in the departments responsible for implementing your project and choose a commonly occurring name from those groups. Or at the very least tally up the most commonly occurring initial amongst the group and use that as a basis for your project name. Pharmaceutical sales executives might review the names of heavy prescribers and note that, when the time comes to release their next blockbuster drug, visiting Dr. Painton early on in the launch of Painaway could prove to be a shrewd move.

Such moves could be the small BIGs that make your *name-changing* activities *game-changing* ones, too.

## CHAPTER 6

# What SMALL steps can lead to BIG leaps when building relationships, partnerships, and teamwork?

Business rarely stands still, and when change happens, it can often occur at lightning speed, throwing unexpected challenges in our way. A sudden acquisition can mean that today's competitor will be tomorrow's colleague. A change in a business model can result in a long-standing rival emerging as the perfect joint venture partner. A seemingly straightforward company restructure can lead to the merging of departments that previously didn't see eye-to-eye.

Marriages like these can be challenging at the best of times. And even more so if those concerned have previously gone to great lengths to differentiate themselves from an adversary that they now find to be an associate. So when a wedding of opponents occurs, what small steps can be taken that will encourage people to accept former rivals as part of the new family, cooperate with new colleagues, work collaboratively, and embrace joint efforts?

One potential answer comes from another group of individuals who are notorious for their fierce rivalries—sports fans.

Rivalry and competitiveness is par for the course in sport. It's something that pretty much every fan recognizes, with the fiercest of cases reserved for the longest standing of foes. Think the Yankees and the Red Sox. The Celtics and the Lakers.

Barcelona and Real Madrid. The Chicago Bears and the Green Bay Packers.

The intensity can be such that it's hard to imagine that rivals like these would be willing to cooperate on anything. But a wonderful series of studies by British psychologist Mark Levine suggests that even in the most extreme of cases, there are some things that bind rather than divide us.

Levine first asked a group of English soccer fans, who happened to be staunch Manchester United supporters, to complete a questionnaire asking them to write down what they liked about their team. After completing the questionnaire, they were then asked to walk to another building on the university campus to take part in the next stage of the study. En route to the building, the Manchester United supporters witnessed a passing jogger (who was actually part of the study) tripping and seemingly injuring themself. Sometimes the jogger would be wearing a plain white shirt. At other times, he was wearing a Manchester United football shirt. And sometimes the jogger was wearing (rather bravely in our opinion) the shirt of Manchester United's fiercest rival, Liverpool.

Strategically placed observers, clipboards at the ready, stood by to count how many of the Manchester United supporters stopped and helped. It turns out that, if you go out jogging and are unlucky enough to sustain an injury, the shirt you are wearing can have a pretty big influence over whether you receive any help. In the study, about a third of the Manchester United supporters stopped to help when the injured jogger wore the plain white t-shirt. As you would have guessed, when they saw that the injured party was one of their own and wearing a Manchester United shirt, the overwhelming majority helped.

But what happened when the jogger wore the shirt of rival club Liverpool? Very few Manchester United fans stopped to help, providing strong evidence of people's tendency to help most those they see as belonging to their immediate in-group.

Happily though, a small change in circumstances can make people much more open to assisting and accommodating those that they initially see as outsiders. When the study was repeated and Manchester United supporters were first asked what they liked about being soccer supporters rather than just what they liked about their team, they were twice as likely to help someone wearing a rival shirt.

So the small BIG here is that, when it comes to encouraging cooperation and partnership, focusing on shared identities becomes important. As a result, managers and leaders looking to encourage an atmosphere of cooperation and support amongst their teams would be advised to take extra time to focus attention on the things that their teams share. On what binds, rather than what divides them.

But is there a way for us to maximize the favorable impact of similarities? Yes.

Adam Grant, a professor at the Wharton School of Business and author of the acclaimed bestseller *Give and Take*, suggests a solution that requires a simple shift in the *type* of commonality to which we direct our efforts.

Instead of asking people to focus on the common similarities that they share with new colleagues, new teams, and new department members, he instead advises that they identify and highlight *uncommon* commonalities. That is, they focus on those features they share in common with a new colleague that are rare to other external groups. Identifying these uncommon commonalities—especially early in the process of relationship building—potentially fulfills people's desire both to fit in and, yet, to stand out (in this case, from other competitive groups) at the same time.

One way that managers can help to draw out these uncommon commonalities would be to encourage team members to fill out getting-to-know-you forms before any formal work is done. Note that it would probably be a mistake to ask questions like, "Name your favorite TV show" or "List your favorite travel destination," because any similarities that are discovered are likely to be fairly common. Instead the advice is to ask team members to make lists that are, say, five or ten items long. In the case of favorite TV shows it is much more likely that, with the longer lists, team members will find that their colleagues also enjoy some of the same undiscovered or ratings-challenged shows that they too enjoy.

Whether it is a simple department restructure or the merging of two industry giants, it takes time for the dust of major change to settle. It seems that the act of encouraging newly formed team members to actively seek out examples of uncommon commonalities, while small, could prove to be a big step that speeds up cooperation, collaboration, and partnership.

## CHAPTER 7

# What SMALL BIG can help you to become wiser with experience?

*The Newlywed Game* is an American game show that first aired in 1966. Given that nearly five decades later it's still going strong in syndicated reruns, the show, in which newly married couples answer a series of increasingly revealing questions about each other to demonstrate how well they know each other (or not), clearly hit on a winning formula.*

The ability to predict people's preferences, wants, and needs is not a skill solely limited to the domains of TV shows like the *Newlywed Game*. It can be an important part of any influence strategy, too. It can also be challenging, especially during the early stages of a relationship when relatively little may be known about your influence target's likes, dislikes, and preferences. Fortunately, any concerns about the shortcomings that exist in our knowledge of new customers and clients will surely be allayed by the feeling that we have comprehensive knowledge

---

*As an aside, one of our favorite clips from the long-running series is when the host asked the wives to predict how their husbands responded to the following question: "Where would you say is the weirdest place that you've ever had the urge to make whoopee?" The husband's answer was "In the car." Her answer? "In the ass!" Suffice it to say, it didn't make it on TV at the time, but it certainly made it to the blooper reel!

about our longer-term ones, those folks with whom we have interacted and done business over time. And one of the major benefits of developing longer-term relationships and arranging regular contact with people is that it seemingly becomes easier to predict their needs and preferences over time.

But it turns out that this might not always be the case. Even in situations where we have known someone for a long time and claim to be pretty good at predicting their likes, dislikes, needs, and preferences, sometimes we are anything but good. In fact, there is evidence to suggest that the longer we know someone, the less likely it is that we will be able to accurately predict their preferences.

In one series of studies by behavior scientists Benjamin Scheibehenne, Jutta Mata, and Peter Todd, people were asked to rate 118 different items on a scale of 1 (don't like it at all) to 4 (like it very much). In addition, these same people were also asked to predict how a person with whom they shared a relationship would rate those same 118 items. Some people in the study were asked to make preference predictions for people they had known for a relatively short time (the average relationship length in this group was around two years) and others were asked to make predictions for those that they had known for much longer (the average relationship length in this group was over ten years).

The 4-point scale that the researchers employed was an important part of the study because it meant that a complete stranger completing the questions could, on average, be expected to get 25 percent of their predictions correct just by chance. Fortunately, and one suspects to everyone's relief, both groups in the study were able to predict the likes and dislikes of someone they knew better than a complete stranger could.

But…not *that* much better.

Those who were asked to predict the preferences of people they had known for an average of two years were accurate 42 percent of the time. Amazingly, those who predicted the preferences of someone whom they had known for over ten years didn't fare nearly as well, with an accuracy rate of just 36 percent.

But perhaps the most telling result of all was how little awareness anyone had of how little they actually knew about people. In the pre-study tests that the researchers conducted, both groups believed that they would be able to predict the likes, dislikes, and preferences with at least 60 percent accuracy. Of course the question to ask at this point is why.

It turns out that there are potentially several reasons why having a longer-standing relationship with another person could lead to *reduced* rather than *increased* levels of understanding of their likes, dislikes, and preferences. One obvious explanation concerns the fact that a large amount of our learning and knowledge exchanges with others occurs in the early stages of relationships, when the motivation to get to know each other is quite high. As time passes, so might those higher levels of motivation, with the result that exchanges of new information occur less regularly. Therefore, some changes in a person's circumstances and situations could go unnoticed.

Another potential explanation for why people in longer-term relationships are sometimes less able to predict a partner's preferences is that people in long-standing relationships typically consider themselves to be more committed to each other by virtue of the extended time they have each invested. As a result, they may think that they know each other better than is actually the case and consequently become less likely to notice changes in attitudes and preferences, especially those that occur slowly or subtly.

There is also evidence to suggest that, in some instances, people who have developed longer-term relationships may be tempted to tell white lies to each other or avoid frank and candid conversations. The telling of white lies and the avoidance of candid conversations could serve to fulfill an important relationship protection function and, in that context, is understandable. However, strategies that serve to protect long-term relationships could lead to a decline in understanding and a dilution of knowledge that could serve to damage the relationship. So while it might be the case that getting older may lead us to be wiser in some domains, such wisdom doesn't necessarily extend to relationships, unless a process is put in place to ensure a continuous and honest exchange of likes, dislikes, and preferences with those with whom we share long-term relationships. Such a process seems not only sensible but healthy too.

Such an approach could also help in your business interactions. Imagine someone who works in a business development role selling their company's services to purchasing managers. Alternatively, imagine an account manager working in a services agency. In both cases it is likely that the people working in these roles will have already invested large amounts of time and effort in order to establish productive and profitable relationships with their customers. It is also possible that folks who work in these sorts of roles will prefer to be the single point of contact for their customers and clients. After all, they know best.

But this research suggests that occasionally inviting a colleague who knows the client less well to meetings could lead to the uncovering of some big new opportunities because that colleague might well end up asking new questions that the experienced executive or manager would not be able to ask without losing credibility, as they would be expected to already know the answers.

Similarly, training departments in customer-centric organizations could arrange for new recruits to work-shadow not only the organization's *best* performers but also the organization's *longest-standing* performers, potentially realizing two benefits. The new recruit would gain valuable experience interacting with customers, and the longer-standing employee would gain valuable new insights from a customer they may have known for many years. The small BIG is that regardless of whether you are interacting with a long-standing customer or a longtime business partner, the importance of arranging for regular exchanges of new information and informal catch-ups cannot be overstated.

## CHAPTER 8

# What SMALL BIGs can persuade people to keep their appointments with you?

L et me see," said the health center manager, reading from a sheet of paper. "Last month we had 353 and the month before that 309. They usually average around 300 a month I suppose. It can be a real problem."

She was talking about patient "no-shows"—or DNAs (Did Not Attends) as they are more commonly known in healthcare industry parlance—people who schedule an appointment and then fail to show up. It turns out that the problem of people failing to attend appointments isn't just limited to inner city health centers or, more broadly, the healthcare industry. As noted in this book's introduction millions of business meetings, hairdresser appointments, restaurant reservations, sales presentations, and student tutorials are missed every year. On a micro level one missed restaurant booking doesn't seem like that big a deal—small potatoes even! But the theme of this book is how small things can make for big differences, and when it comes to missed appointments the costs can add up to staggering sums of money. Recall in our introduction how health economists in the UK have estimated that the overall cost of people failing to show for health appointments is £800 million (that's over a billion US dollars) every year. That's money being poured down the drain simply because individuals fail to live up to their commitments.

Also in the introduction we suggested that there are ways of persuading people to keep their appointments, and more generally to live up to their commitments, simply by making a couple of small, costless changes in approach that can lead to some pretty dramatic improvements.

One of the fundamental principles of social influence involves the relationship between commitment and consistency. This principle describes a deeply held motivation that most of us have to behave consistently with the previous commitments we have made, especially those commitments that are active, require effort on our part, and that are made public to others.

To give an example, researchers posing as visitors to a beach would place a beach towel and a radio on the sand in close view of a sunbather before heading down to the shore to take a dip in the sea. In one condition, one of the researchers would ask the sunbather (who was really the subject of the study) to watch the radio. Most agreed and verbally signaled their commitment with a friendly, "Of course I will." In a second condition the researcher simply went for a swim without making any kind of request of the sunbather. Then the real experiment began. Another researcher, posing as an opportunistic thief, would run past, snatching up the radio and making off with it. The small act of asking for a verbal commitment made a big difference as to whether sunbathers who witnessed the fake theft gave chase. Only 4 out of 20 of those who weren't asked to make a verbal commitment made any attempt to right the wrong. Contrast that with the 19 out of 20 sunbathers who were asked to watch the radio and who, consequently, leapt into action. Why? Because they had verbally agreed to a commitment, and giving chase was entirely consistent with that previous verbal commitment.

If a small change such as asking for a verbal commitment could be employed to such impressive effect to reduce theft at the beach, one wonders whether a similar strategy could be used to reduce appointment no-shows at the medical center.

In an attempt to answer this question, we conducted a series of experiments in three busy doctors' offices where patients, immediately after being provided with a date and time in a standard appointment-making call, were asked to read back out loud those appointment details before hanging up the phone. This small change proved to have a modest effect when we measured the impact on subsequent no-show rates, reducing them by just over 3 percent. At first glance this doesn't appear to be that big a difference until one considers two important factors. First, the strategy was costless to implement, adding at most a second or two to the interaction. Second, even though the 3 percent reduction appears to be relatively small, in terms of scale it is actually quite large. A 3 percent reduction such as this applied to a $1 billion problem would save $30 million.

The implication is clear. It is all too easy in our busy lives to cut short one interaction or conversation so that we can then focus our attention on the next. To do so without seeking some sort of verbal commitment of what has been agreed is an opportunity wasted, even if that opportunity is likely to spawn seemingly modest results. For example, a manager might garner greater commitment to solid actions from a team meeting if the individual members vocalized them at the end of the meeting. A parent might reduce those stressful bedtime negotiations by seeking a verbal agreement before agreeing to just one more game or story or TV program.

It turns out that sometimes these verbal commitments don't have to be fully explicit either. For example a business development manager hoping to persuade a prospect to attend a meeting to hear an industry speaker could increase the chances that he or she will attend by asking them to submit a question for the Q&A session. Eliciting a question in advance from a prospect can act as a small commitment that potentially increases the likelihood that they will subsequently attend the event.

These are all examples of how requesting a simple verbal commitment could be a costless small BIG that improves your chances for effective influence. But might there be an even better way to secure future commitments from others? It turns out that there is, and to understand what it is we need to return to the doctor's office.

One common strategy that we noticed all the health centers in our study utilizing was to provide patients with an appointment card with the time and date of their next appointment. Usually, the appointment details were written out by a health-care receptionist. We wondered whether this approach was unwise, given that the principle of consistency states that people are most motivated to be consistent with those commitments that they actively make themselves.

Accordingly, we tested the impact of another small change—one that served to actively, rather than passively, involve the patient in the appointment-making process. What was this small change? It was for the receptionist to simply ask the patient to write down the time and date of the next appointment on the card *themselves*. When we tested this approach over a four-month period, we measured a significant, 18 percent reduction in no-shows in that group. A small BIG that, if scaled up properly, could now result in savings not of $30 million, but of $180 million. All done at a cost of, well, zero.

This additional insight from our doctors' studies shines a spotlight on another important but undernoticed trap that we often fall into in the course of modern-day interactions and meetings: How easy it is to default to doing things ourselves in the knowledge that at least they will get done. As a result, a salesperson leaving a meeting might find that she has many subsequent actions to undertake, yet her customer has relatively few or even none at all. In such a context it is likely that the salesperson will be much more committed than the customer to the sales process itself. A personal trainer might believe that writing up his client's tailored exercise program demonstrates how attentive, focused, and service-oriented he is, but maybe misses the point that the client is potentially less committed to the program.

But what about instances when it is unrealistic to expect a potential client or customer to make active and written commitments? Or how about those meetings where multiple people attend, and it would be unwise to share actions across the group, or unfair to nominate one person to take total responsibility? In situations like these it is probably better to write up all the actions and then circulate them yourself, ensuring that you make a small but crucial addition to the top of your email. Asking recipients to signal by way of a simple "yes" response that the notes you have sent are an accurate reflection of *their* understanding of next steps is a good start.

But sometimes, no matter how hard we try, our persuasion attempts can fall short. In such situations, what other small changes, linked to the commitment and consistency principle, might we employ?

## CHAPTER 9

# What SMALL BIG can help your influence attempts to win over and over?

Readers of our previous book, *Yes! 50 Secrets from the Science of Persuasion* (and there are now over half a million), will be familiar with a series of studies that two of us conducted with our colleague Vlad Griskevicius, in which we looked at how a small change to the wording on the card that hotels use to persuade guests to reuse their towels can make a big difference in whether that guest actually does so. (For those readers who aren't familiar with that study, towel reuse rose by 26 percent when the words on the card were changed to honestly point out that the majority of previous guests do reuse their towels.)

Given that these little cards are familiar to the millions of people who regularly stay in hotels, these studies spark lots of debate and discussion when we present them in workshops and talks. Sometimes someone will ask us about other potential strategies that hotel managers might employ in an attempt to persuade guests to reuse their towels and linens. For example, could asking guests to make a small commitment before they even reach their guest room, such as at the check-in desk, have an influence on their likelihood to behave in an environmentally beneficial way?

It turns out that another team of persuasion scientists has been testing this exact idea. They found that by simply asking guests to make what seems like a small commitment when they check-in to a hotel can lead to some big differences, not only in increasing towel and linen reuse but to other positive beneficial outcomes, too.

Over a one-month period, researcher Katie Baca-Motes and her colleagues arranged for guests checking in to a popular California hotel to be asked to make a commitment related to environmental protection. In some instances the commitment requested was a general one, asking guests to check a box indicating their willingness to be environmentally protective during their stay. In other instances the commitment requested was a more specific one, namely to check a box indicating their willingness to reuse their towels during their stay.

In addition to asking for either a general or a specific commitment, some guests were given a "Friends of the Earth" pin badge. As a control, these badges were also given to a number of other guests who had not been asked to make a commitment when they checked into the hotel.

Finally, another control group of guests were simply checked in in the normal fashion and were not given a pin badge or asked to make any kind of a commitment.

So what happened?

The first thing that the study looked at was the percentage of guests who were actually willing to make a commitment. That number turned out to be very high. Some 98 percent of guests in the general commitment group were willing to make a commitment, and even though the number of guests willing to make a more specific commitment was lower, it was still impressive, with 83 percent checking the box. So, at first glance, it seems that when attempting to persuade an individual to make a commitment, you might increase your chances of success by asking them to make a general rather than a more specific commitment.

Of course, this leads us to ask another question. Which commitments are more likely to be lived up to: general commitments or specific ones?

The researchers found that the guests who made a specific commitment at check-in were more likely to reuse their towels than the guests who made a general commitment (66 percent versus 61 percent). Perhaps more interestingly, those guests who did make a specific commitment to reuse their towels were also much more likely to adopt other environmentally protective behaviors consistent with their initial commitment. For example, they were more likely to turn off the lights when they left their room as well as turn down the air conditioning unit and switch off the TV as they vacated. This finding is quite counter-intuitive; after all, one could easily imagine that those who make a general commitment to protect the environment would engage in more environmentally friendly behaviors than those who simply committed to reusing towels.

What's the small BIG insight here? Anyone facing the challenge of persuading people to make multiple, related changes in their behaviors should be able to maximize results with a small two-step approach. Step one is to ensure that the initial commitments sought are specific ones. Step two is to make sure the environment where that commitment will be performed includes cues that act as triggers for other *related* and desirable behaviors wholly consistent with the initial specific commitment.

Let's take an example. Imagine that as the manager of an office facility you have the challenge of not only encouraging more recycling but also reducing your general energy costs. This finding suggests that you should first ask office workers to make a specific commitment to one behavior (let's say, to place paper in the recycling bin as they leave the office at night) and then position cues in a place that could activate related behaviors that will reduce energy costs (let's say, place the recycling bins next to a light switch). Doing this potentially creates a "two outcomes for the price of one request" influence strategy that could be boosted further if a small card is placed next to the lights reminding workers "Don't forget your commitment to the environment. Please turn off the lights." This extra step is important as you will see in the next chapter.

But before we get ahead of ourselves let's find out what happened to those hotel guests who were given one of those pin badges. As you might expect, guests who made a little (checkmark) commitment and who were also given a badge were even more likely to reuse their towels than those that had just made the commitment. They were also the most likely to engage in other environmentally protective behaviors while staying in the hotel, suggesting that these little badges provided two important features. They served both as a reminder to the individual of their commitment and as a signal to others of their commitment. The impact of this small badge serves as a useful reminder that it is not enough for charities to simply encourage people to make a donation to their cause. It is also vital that they provide some form of public sign—for example, a lapel badge, a window card, or a bumper sticker—that signals their commitment.

But what about those hotel guests who had a pin badge thrust on them *without* having first made a little commitment to the environment? They were the least likely of all to reuse their towels—even less likely, in fact, than the guests who weren't part of the study at all.

This is consistent with previous research that has repeatedly shown that for a commitment to stand the best chance of being lived up to, it needs to be *owned* by the person making that commitment. There was certainly no sense of ownership in the case of hotel guests who had pin badges pushed upon them. Quite the opposite.

In fact there are two other aspects that are also crucial ingredients to the likelihood of a commitment made being fulfilled: how action-oriented that commitment is and how publicly it is made by the person or group committing to it. When hotel staff thrust badges onto guests they were eliminating the opportunity for guests to take an action themselves, and in doing so removed any element of choice over guests' public commitments. It was this two-sided error that contributed to the disastrous results measured.

Of course, it is rare for a business to want to influence only people outside their organization, such as customers and clients. Invariably some of their challenges will concern persuading people on the inside—their employees and associates—to change their behaviors too.

This was certainly the case with the hotel in this study whose housekeeping staff would often replace towels even if guests had indicated that they wished to reuse them. But perhaps the best strategy to persuade housekeeping staff to comply with appropriate towel replacement is the same that was used to persuade guests to comply with appropriate towel reuse—specifically, that the hotel manager should first seek a small voluntary commitment, such as asking housekeeping staff how important they believe it is for hotel staff to listen to guests' wishes. Once this has been done, the manager could then suggest that one way housekeeping staff can demonstrate that they are listening would be to rehang towels when a guest indicates their desire to reuse them. Of course the hotel manager should avoid mandating that housekeeping staff wear "We listen to our guests" badges and instead offer them the chance to voluntarily wear them.

Who knows, if they do, they might even turn the lights off as they leave.

## CHAPTER 10

# What SMALL BIG can ensure your influence attempts don't backfire?

You do your best to recycle whenever you can, right? Maybe the company you work for has a pro-environmental policy that encourages staff to use less paper and to recycle as much of it as possible. It certainly wouldn't be alone. Increasing numbers of organizations and communities are recognizing the benefits of recycling as a way to conserve natural resources.

But could certain strategies designed to persuade people to recycle actually be *counterproductive*, leading to an *increase* rather than a *decrease* in the use of resources? Persuasion researchers think that this kind of backfire effect can occur under certain conditions. That has important implications not just for your office's environmental policy but for your wider influence attempts, too.

Influence rarely occurs in a vacuum, and one possible implication of focusing attention on a single specific behavior is that it might lead to unintended, even counterproductive behaviors down the line. You can probably think of examples from your personal life. Spending an extra ten minutes on the treadmill to feel a little fitter might also persuade you that you have earned the right to that tasty muffin to accompany your morning coffee. Selecting the healthy salad at lunch might "buy" you the right to a dessert, or at least entitle you to take the elevator instead of the stairs when returning to your desk after lunch.

Behavioral scientists Jesse Catlin and Yitong Wang wondered if this "licensing" effect—essentially, when engaging in one positive behavior licenses you to slack off on another positive behavior—might also occur when it comes to encouraging people to behave in environmentally responsible ways. For example, could providing recycling facilities in an attempt to encourage people to recycle and dispose of paper towels more responsibly actually cause people to use even *more* resources than they would if recycling facilities weren't available?

In order to test this idea, the researchers designed two studies. In the first study participants were told that they would be evaluating a new brand of scissors. Part of the evaluation process required them to rate how good the scissors were at cutting out shapes (such as triangles and squares) from a stack of approximately 200 sheets of plain white paper. Half the participants tested the scissors in a room where there weren't any recycling facilities, only a trash can. The other half completed the task in a room where recycling facilities were available in addition to a regular trash can. The participants were purposely not given any specific instructions about the sizes of the shapes or the amount of paper that they should use in the task. Instead they were simply told to dispose of any scraps in the receptacle(s) provided. Then they completed a "green attitude" questionnaire that asked them about their beliefs and attitudes toward the environment.

The results were quite simply staggering. Participants who evaluated the pair of scissors when recycling facilities were available used *nearly three times* more paper than the group who didn't have recycling facilities. Interestingly, this increase in the use of resources occurred regardless of how positive the participants' "green attitudes" were, as measured in the post-study questionnaire.

So this first study demonstrated a clear case of licensing; the presence of paper-recycling facilities caused people to actually use more—not less—paper. One potential criticism of studies like these is that because they are conducted in a laboratory setting, the results may not reflect what happens in the real world. So Catlin and Wang transported their studies out of the university lab and set them up...in a men's restroom!

Before starting out on this change of venue, they first collected data on the amount of paper hand towels used in the men's restroom for a period of 15 days to work out the average amount of paper towels typically used each day. Once this had been done they then introduced a large recycling bin near the sinks with signs indicating that the restrooms were participating in a paper hand towel recycling program, and that any used hand towels placed in the bin would be recycled. For the next 15 days, they then simply measured the amount of paper hand towels used.

Consistent with their laboratory studies, paper towel usage increased after the introduction of the recycling bin by an average of half a paper towel per person. At first glance this small increase doesn't seem that big a deal. However, given that the restroom was typically used over a hundred times each work day, the increase in usage was substantial: It totaled about 12,500 paper hand towels annually for this one restroom alone. The presence of recycling facilities led to an increase, not a decrease, in the use of resources. And in a big way!

So what's going on? One possible explanation involves guilt. That is, if people experience a feeling of guilt when consuming and disposing of products, they may feel that by recycling them they can reduce any negative feelings associated with over-consumption. Of course that subsequent reduction in negative feeling might now license them to consume even more because their overconsumption will be mitigated by recycling.

Or perhaps the availability of the recycling option serves as a simple justification cue. Maybe people are saying to themselves "Hey if it can be recycled then it probably doesn't matter if I use a little bit more."

Regardless of the psychological mechanism that is providing people with this license, one implication is immediately clear. When seeking to persuade people to behave in environmentally desirable ways, providing facilities that make it easy for people to do so, while vital, may simply not be enough to achieve the desired outcome—particularly in situations where there is little or no cost to the user of the resource that is being consumed. This was certainly the case in the paper recycling studies, and it might be the case when it comes to influencing your colleagues and coworkers in the office, too.

An example is in order. Imagine for a few moments that you have been "lucky" enough to be volunteered as the new Green Champion in your office, and you now have the not-so-enviable challenge of persuading your coworkers to use a little less paper, recycle the paper they do use, and adopt some other environmentally friendly practices like turning out the lights when they leave the building. Imagine further that arrangements have been made for facilities such as recycling boxes to be strategically placed around the building and for energy-efficient bulbs to be installed in the light fixtures. Knowing that these facilities, while essential, might also have the unintended consequence of licensing your colleagues to use more rather than less resources, you recognize the need to make some additional small steps to mitigate any potential licensing effects. So what might they be?

Well, the first step might be to add a sign at recycling points and light switches, pointing out that while recycling is beneficial to the environment, using fewer resources in the first place is even more beneficial. Doing so would be consistent with emerging research that has shown that while the benefits of recycling are often highly salient to people, the cost of recycling is much less so.

Another potential step would be to take an insight from the commitment and consistency principle and highlight the commitments and promises that individuals may have previously made toward environmental protection. Better still, you might seek small commitments from people prior to starting the program. Recall from chapter 9 the studies carried out in hotels, in which asking guests to sign a pledge when they checked into the hotel not only led to an increase in towel and linen reuse, but also caused guests to be more likely to turn off the lights and TV when they left their rooms. That's an example of a "positive spillover" effect.

A well-established first-order law of behavior-change programs is to "make change easy for people." Studies like these add a caveat: providing facilities that make change easy for people, while crucial, won't always be enough. The effective influencer will also consider potential licensing effects and include small steps to eliminate them that lead to big successes with their strategies.

## CHAPTER 11

# What SMALL BIG should you add to your recipe for employee productivity?*

*Preparation time: five minutes*

E ncouraging employees to be productive workers can be a challenge for even the best managers. Fortunately many managers will have a range of tools at their disposal in their motivational toolbox. For example, one of the more common ways to increase worker motivation is to simply offer to pay more to workers who are especially productive. Alternatively managers can try to enhance overall employee morale by including them in a profit-sharing program. Or perhaps managers can provide recognition to the best workers by offering desirable rewards such as iPhones, weekend breaks, or even lunch with the CEO.

Although all of these tactics have the potential to be effective, they also share some downsides. For example financial incentives have a tendency to set new reference points for the future. An employee who has been paid an incentive for performing a task once is then likely to expect that similar incentive payments will be forthcoming in the future, and with a subsequent lowering of motivation levels when they are not. Financial incentives can also sometimes serve to erode any intrinsic motivation employees have to perform in that manner anyway. But probably most important of all is the simple fact that incentives can be expensive to implement.

However, research from behavioral science suggests that

adding a single ingredient to the productivity recipe can improve the result and will do so at no cost. What's more, all that's required is one small change that will take just five easy minutes.

Remember Adam Grant, the Wharton School of Business professor who we mentioned in chapter 6? He believed that workers often fail to live up to their potential due to one fundamental ingredient that is missing: They've lost track of the significance and meaningfulness of their jobs. Grant figured that if employees could be reminded of why their jobs are important, they might become more highly motivated and, as a result, become more productive individuals.

To test this idea, he set up a study in the call center of a university whose employees were tasked with contacting alumni and persuading them to make donations to the college's scholarship funds. Grant first randomly divided the call center employees into three groups. Employees assigned to the first group read stories written by other employees that described what those employees perceived were the personal benefits of the job. Typically they would write about the financial package they received and the opportunities the job gave them for the development of their own personal skills and knowledge. Grant refers to this group as the "personal benefit" condition.

However, another set of employees read stories written by students who had benefited from the organization's fundraising activities. These were individuals who described how the scholarships they obtained had an enormously positive impact on their lives, giving them a way to achieve treasured goals and dreams that would have been otherwise unattainable. Grant refers to this group as the "task significance" condition.

Finally, as a control condition, the last group of employees did not read any stories at all. Grant subsequently measured the number of pledges earned as well as the amount of donation money obtained by all the callers both one week prior to the study and one month afterward.

What he found was simply amazing.

Employees in the "personal benefit" and control conditions performed almost exactly the same after the intervention as they did before it both in terms of the amount of donation money they raised and the number of pledges they earned. Yet, those in the "task significance" condition earned *more than twice* the number of weekly pledges, going from an average of 9 to an average of 23. They also raised more than twice the amount of money, with average weekly donations growing from $1,288 a week to $3,130.

So what was it about this particular approach that was driving such an incredible increase? Further analyses suggested that the increase was due primarily to the fact that previously unmotivated employees were being spurred on by recognizing their connection to the touching personal stories they read. Energized by these results, they were making more calls per hour, speaking to more people, and consequently collecting more donations.

This insight provides a timely lesson for anyone tasked with motivating others. Regardless of whether the work concerns one's role in a private corporation, the public sector, or a social enterprise, there is likely to be some significance and mean-ingfulness in nearly every job. The small change that managers would be advised to make is to take steps to ensure that their employees don't lose sight of what that is.

What are those steps? For businesses that don't already routinely collect customer stories, testimonials, and reports about how an employee, product, or service has benefited them in a positive way, the advice is to start doing so now. For those that already do collect customer stories, perhaps displaying them publicly on bulletin and notice boards is another small change that could have a potentially large impact. Or, rather than leave it to chance that employees will proactively read them, you could take the stories to your staff. In the same way Adam Grant arranged for staff to read stories about the impact their efforts could make, the team leader and supervisors might begin each staff meeting by reviewing a customer account of a job well done. Given some of the insights we have previously discussed on commitment strategies it might even be more powerful to ask team members to pick out their favorite stories and read them out loud to their colleagues rather than a manager reading them.

Another change a savvy manager could make would be to actually ask customers to come and tell their stories so staffs could hear their accounts firsthand. These days, thanks to technology like Skype and FaceTime, this doesn't even require a physical visit to the company's office, so it's fairly easy for workers located in a place like Ames, Iowa, to see the impact they and their products have had on customers in Nairobi, Kenya, for example. Evidence of the potential upsides of this approach comes from a further insight gleaned from Adam Grant's studies—that is, when callers had an opportunity to meet scholarship students face-to-face and hear their stories, it further fueled callers' motivation and success.

The applications of this small BIG are potentially limitless. Pharmaceutical companies, for example, could reconnect their sales representatives to the significance of what they do by arranging for patients to describe how their life has improved as a result of their medication. Social workers and home helpers are likely to feel more appreciated if they learn, firsthand, of the difference they make to people's lives.

Finally, in recounting a story from his experiences in the call center, Grant describe a sad sign he saw above someone's desk. It read "Doing a good job in this place is like wetting your pants in a dark suit. You get a warm feeling no one recognizes." Maybe that's the smallest change of all for a manager to make—to simply say "well done" to an employee who has made a difference.

## CHAPTER 12

# What SMALL BIGs should you look to avoid when it comes to successfully making decisions?

In 1973, Barry Diller, the then VP of prime-time programming at the American Broadcasting Company (ABC), shattered the record for the amount paid for the rights to broadcast a single movie, shelling out $3.3 million to air *The Poseidon Adventure* on TVs around the nation.

This huge sum alone would have been enough to raise many eyebrows ($15.3 million in today's dollars), but even more astonishing was the fact that the moment he put pen to paper, Diller already knew he would be losing at least $1 million on the deal.

So, what would influence a seasoned executive with years of industry experience to pay more than he should have, wanted to, or even needed to? And when it comes to your own negotiations, what small changes can you make that could help you avoid making a similar error?

Let's leave 1970s TV for a few moments and transport ourselves to an entirely different environment—the modern-day business school. On the first day of his negotiating class Max Bazerman, a professor at Harvard Business School, conducts an interesting experiment. He takes a $20 bill from his wallet and offers it up for auction. Anyone is welcome to take part in the auction provided that they abide by the auction's two rules. Bids must be made in $1 increments and the runner-up must, as a penalty, pay an amount equivalent to their last bid while receiving nothing in return. The auction begins and hands quickly go up as people try to seize the opportunity to acquire cash on the cheap. "The pattern is always the same," Bazerman says. "The bidding starts out fast and furious." But then something interesting happens.

As the bids approach the $14–$16 range it suddenly becomes clear to each bidder that he or she isn't the only one hoping to snag a bargain. All of a sudden arms become welded to people's sides and hands are thrust deep into pockets as bidders rapidly retreat, leaving only the two highest offers in the game. At that point something *really* interesting happens. Without realizing it, the two remaining bidders have become locked in a new game. Instead of playing to win, they are now playing *not to lose*.

It is clear to any outsider that the bidders should cut their losses before the auction spins out of control. But they rarely do. Bazerman claims to have conducted over 200 separate auctions and only on one occasion did it end before the bid reached $20. Sometimes his $20 bill sells for over $100. Once, for a record $204!

So what's going on? It appears that during Bazerman's auctions two persuasive elements join forces to influence bidder behavior. The first is commitment and consistency, the idea that once someone makes even a small initial commitment they then encounter personal and interpersonal pressure to behave consistently with that commitment. It is easy to see how, at just $1, the cost of entry to Bazerman's auction is a small enough commitment that most people are willing to make it. No surprise, then, that so many people do put their hands up. That subsequent bids are made only in small increments of a dollar further fuels a bidder's desire for consistency. It is as if they are saying to themselves, "Well I have already bid $1, which is only a small amount, so to raise my offer by another $1 doesn't seem that big a deal." Of course it quickly becomes apparent that many others are in the auction, and recognizing the competition for a scarce resource (remember, only one person can successfully bid for the $20 bill), a second persuasive force comes into play: not so much the desire to win but the more potent need to avoid losing.

And that's essentially what happened to ABC's Diller. On learning that competitor broadcasters also had an interest in purchasing rights for the movie, and having already invested time and resources into winning the bid, not to mention his reputation, Diller could only move in one direction. His subsequent bids continued to escalate, quickly passing the point where he knew he was throwing away his money.

Diller's story exemplifies a trap that many competitive negotiators fall into known as the "escalation of commitment," a condition that is not just limited to individuals. At around the same time that Diller was conducting his negotiations, the Long Island Lighting Company was scheduled to unveil its $70 million nuclear power plant. However, due to a series of costly overruns, and even despite evidence of the plant's economic infeasibility, it would be another decade before they pulled the plug on the project—by which time their costs had spiraled to over $6 billion!

Recognizing that escalations in commitment can often lead to poor outcomes and a potential loss of money and resources, many will adopt strategies designed to mitigate its influence. One of the most common is to arrange for one individual to make the initial decision about whether to enter a negotiation and then assign a different individual to carry out that negotiation. For example, a company looking to procure a new computer software system might delegate the responsibility of choosing that new system to one decision maker, but once a decision has

been made, delegate the next job of negotiating that purchase
to a different person. The thinking here is that by separating
out the decision maker and negotiator roles, any escalations in
commitment and the financial pitfalls that accompany them
can be dodged.

In theory this sounds like a good strategy but it's one that
can sometimes still fail for a very simple but often overlooked
reason. While a separate decision maker / negotiator strategy
removes a *physical* connection between the two parties involved,
it may not serve to remove any *psychological* connections that
may exist. This leads to an intriguing question. Might the negotiator ensnare themselves in the decision maker's commitments
simply because they share a connection with them? And if this
does happen, is the resulting outcome likely to mirror those
experienced by Barry Diller and Max Bazerman's students?

In an attempt to test these ideas, social scientists Brian
Gunia, Niro Sivanathan, and Adam Galinsky set up a series of
studies. In one experiment participants first read an account of
a vice president of finance who had decided to invest $5 million
dollars in the consumer division of his company. They also
learned that over the past five years that division had performed
significantly worse than another division that he chose not to
invest in. The participants were then told to imagine that they
had just been appointed as the new vice president and consider
how they would invest $10 million of new funds. However,
before making their decisions, half of them were to spend a few
minutes engaged in some "perspective-taking" by considering
how the previous VP might have felt and thought as he made
his investment decisions. The other half were simply told to be
objective and not take into account the previous incumbent's
perspective at all.

The results demonstrated that those asked to take the
perspective of the previous VP were not only influenced by the

previous poor decision, they were also more likely to escalate the previous commitment that had been made, typically investing 40 percent more in that division than the control group. Perhaps most interestingly of all, this occurred despite the participants being offered a $50 cash bonus if the decisions that they made led to the best financial outcome.

But hang on a second. Today's fast-paced and competitive business world is hardly conducive to undertaking our own perspective-taking, let alone someone else's. So perhaps the procurement managers and buyers who are tasked with making decisions and negotiating on behalf of their organization can breathe a sigh of relief, confident in the knowledge that, in the absence of any deep connection, their performance is unlikely to be unduly affected.

Further studies by the researchers showed that such confidence might be misplaced. In fact, they found evidence that even seemingly meaningless connections—such as sharing a birth month and graduation year—can be enough to lock individuals into another's commitments.

So what small changes might insights such as these prompt you to make to avoid falling into the trap of being influenced by others' commitments? Imagine that you manage the procurement department in your organization and are responsible for a team of negotiators and purchasers. The results of these studies suggest that you take steps to select the member of your team who, all else being equal, has the fewest connections with the personnel of the department for which you are negotiating.

Managers also might consider the implications of these studies. As tempting as it would be to promote, for example, one of the team's long-standing high performers in your sales department, the connection that individual likely has with the previous sales manager might serve to extend the life of decisions and strategies that you would actually prefer to eliminate. On the other hand, if you want the approaches and strategies employed by a previous manager to continue, then appointing that individual might be exactly the right thing to do.

And of course when it comes to your own negotiations and decisions, an awareness of the small but powerful influences that can sway your actions and decisions is crucial. Acting in accord with this insight might be enough for you to avoid a *Poseidon*-like adventure yourself that leads to the sinking of your business. For instance, research led by Jeffrey Pfeffer of the Graduate School of Business at Stanford University demonstrated that, if you have overseen a particular project within your organization, you would be well advised to assign the job of judging its success to someone else within the organization. That's because you will be inclined to overestimate the project's value—sometimes dramatically. Further, the less connected that selected judge feels to you, the more objective his or her assessment of the project will be.

# CHAPTER 13

# What SMALL BIG is the key to planning persuasion?

"Yes" might just be the most beautiful word in the English language when we're trying to persuade others to take a particular course of action. But oftentimes getting someone to simply say yes to our requests won't be enough to get the job done. This is especially the case when there is a delay between someone agreeing to take action and the point at which the action is actually carried out. Many of us will be able to recall times when a colleague or coworker readily agreed to help us—"Sure I'll bring up your proposal in the meeting next week," or "Of course I'll send that report over to you," or "Leave it to me. I'll happily connect you with the new VP"—only to subsequently fail to deliver on the promise. It's probably not the case that people are paying lip service to your requests (or at least one hopes they are not). It's just that so many other things are vying for their attention that between agreeing to your request and carrying out that task, their initial commitment to you can get crowded out.

Fortunately, persuasion science points the way to a small but often ignored strategy to encourage people to follow through with their initial commitments: Have them form a specific plan for where, when, and how they will go about accomplishing the task to which they have committed. Behavioral scientists call these specific plans *implementation intentions*.

A good illustration of the big differences that can be gained by making a small additional change to help facilitate implementation intention comes from a series of studies conducted by researchers David Nickerson and Todd Rogers. They wanted to know whether asking potential voters to form a specific plan for how they would get to the polls on Election Day would actually influence whether these voters would follow through on their intention to vote. To answer this question, they conducted an experiment in which a large sample of individuals eligible to vote in the 2008 presidential primary were called at home using one of several different scripts.

The first script was the "Standard Script," which sought to encourage people to vote by reminding them about the election and informing them that voting is an important responsibility. The second script, the "Self-Prediction Script," was essentially the same as the Standard Script with the addition of a question that simply asked whether the person intended to vote. This Self-Prediction Script was based on previous research suggesting that asking people to predict whether they will perform a socially desirable behavior increases the likelihood that they'll do so by encouraging them to say yes, which then leads them to feel committed to that course of action.

The third script, however—the "Voting Plan Script"— was identical to the Self-Prediction Script but included three follow-up questions designed to encourage those individuals who signaled their intention to vote to create a voting plan on the spot. These questions were, "What time will you vote?" "Where will you be coming from?" and "What will you be doing beforehand?" The central idea was that by answering these specific questions, individuals would more easily generate a concrete plan that would take into consideration all of their other obligations that day and that it would be easier for them to follow through come Election Day. Finally, there was a control condition that did not involve any contact with the potential voters whatsoever.

Realizing that asking people to report whether or not they voted after the election could produce a whole host of biases and inaccurate data, the researchers instead examined the official voter turnout records to see who did and did not end up actually voting in the election. The results clearly showed that the most effective script was the Voting Plan Script, which increased turnout by more than 4 percentage points compared to control. What's more, the researchers found that this script had the most impact among households in which there was only a single eligible voter, increasing their turnout by 9.1 percentage points.

Although there are several possible explanations, the evidence appears consistent with the possibility that multiple-eligible-voter households are much more likely to spontaneously generate concrete voting plans than single-eligible-voter households because they have more schedules to juggle. That suggests that the single-eligible-voter households have more of an opportunity to benefit from being asked to generate a plan by an outside party than do multiple-eligible-voter households.

It's clearly evident from this research that simply hearing "yes" from another person is often the starting point, rather than the ending point, for persuasion. To optimize the likelihood that people will follow through with their intentions, it is necessary to consider asking a couple of extra and specific questions about how they plan to go about accomplishing the goal they've promised to pursue.

This doesn't need to be done in a micromanaging or demanding way. In fact, the questions could simply relate to small details or specific aspects of the task. For example, the leader of a weight loss club could, at the end of each session, gently inquire about how her members will be getting to the next session, what time they will leave work, and if they have made arrangements to have their children looked after. She might even share these implementation intention plans with other members, with two additional benefits. The implementation plans are made public to others (nicely aligning to the commitment and consistency principle), and members might uncover information about each other that cements future commitments—for example, two members realizing that they live close by each other and therefore could travel together to future sessions.

In a slightly different vein, staff members might improve their effectiveness in persuading colleagues from other departments to attend a regular weekly meeting by making a small change to the standard question "Are you able to attend the meeting at 4 p.m. this Wednesday?" and ask instead, "What are your plans just before this Wednesday's 4 p.m. meeting?"

The remarkable impact made by a small change to a question asked has also been demonstrated in a study designed to help people get back to work. Recognizing that claimants who visited job centers would typically be asked what job-seeking activities they had conducted in the two previous weeks, the question was changed to direct their attention to a future implementation intention: "What activities will you undertake in the next fortnight that could help you to secure a job?" The study, conducted by the UK government's Behavioural Insight Team, provides an excellent example of a small change resulting in a big difference. In a three-month trial period, jobseekers who were asked to form implementation intention plans were up to 20 percent more likely to be off unemployment benefits after 13 weeks than jobseekers in a control group that was asked the standard question.

This persuasion strategy has been used to promote another really important behavior: immunization. Behavioral scientist

Katherine Milkman and her colleagues conducted a study at a large company offering free flu vaccinations to its employees. In this experiment, all eligible employees received a mailing reminding them to get a flu vaccination at one of the company's on-site clinics, and that reminder included dates and locations of those clinics. There were two additional conditions to this study. In the first condition the reminder card prompted employees to write down the date that they were planning to get the flu shot. The second condition was similar to the first condition but took the implementation intentions one step further: In this condition, the reminder card not only asked for the date but also the *time* that the employee was planning to get the flu shot. The researchers found that the reminder card that prompted employees to write down just the date boosted flu vaccinations by 1.5 percentage points relative to the standard control message. But the card that prompted the more specific information—both the date and the time—resulted in a boost of flu vaccinations by 4.2 percentage points.

Although these percentage increases may seem small, consider the big difference they could make in a large multinational company: The vaccinations could prevent these employees not only from having to endure the flu, but also from passing it around the office, infecting others. What's more, this study is especially interesting in that, unlike the other implementation intention studies we described above, the employees were asked to state (or in this case, to write down) their intentions in private rather than in public. While the studies we have previously discussed typically advocate commitments that are made publicly, this study suggests that even commitments made privately can be effective, demonstrating the versatility of this persuasion strategy.

## CHAPTER 14

## What SMALL BIG can lock people into your persuasion attempts?

Sometimes, no matter how hard we try and no matter how well informed we are about how to persuade others effectively, our strategies will fall short. There can be dozens of reasons why an otherwise properly employed influence strategy fails to yield the desired results when trying to convince people to do something they *should*, but do not necessarily *want*, to do. Regardless of whether you're trying to convince someone to support your favorite charity, eat healthier, switch their business from their current supplier to your firm, or just adopt a new way of working at the office, one of the most common explanations for lack of persuasive success is also one of the simplest: People recognize they should change their behavior, but they just don't feel like doing it *right now.*

Research conducted by social psychologists like Dan Gilbert, Yaacov Trope, and Nira Liberman suggests that people typically think about events that occur in the *near future* and events that occur in the *distant future* quite differently. Whereas individuals tend to think about near future events in very concrete terms, they are much more likely to think about events that seem far off in the future in more abstract terms. For example, if you were to ask your coworkers to volunteer for a weekend at a local homeless shelter, their evaluations of that task are likely to differ depending on whether you're asking them to help out this upcoming weekend or on a weekend eight months from now. If you are asking them about the upcoming weekend, they are likely to focus on the concrete costs they will incur if they agree to volunteer—for instance, they won't have the opportunity to go shopping, they might miss the weekend's big game on ESPN, or they'll simply lose the chance to catch up on some sleep.

On the other hand, if you are asking your coworkers to volunteer on a weekend eight months from now, they are more likely to evaluate your proposition at a much more general level, including how the request relates to their own general values, morals, and ideologies. Therefore, those considering the request to volunteer many months from now are less likely to ask themselves whether they *want* to do it and more likely to ask themselves whether they *should* do it. With the subsequent realization that being helpful is consistent with their values, they become more likely to say yes to that request and follow through on that commitment.

Behavioral scientists Todd Rogers and Max Bazerman call this commitment strategy "future lock-in," and deploying it requires making a small but important change in your approach. Rather than asking people to agree to a change right away, you should ask them to agree to a change that will be implemented at some point in the future—assuming of course that it is a change that benefits them and ideally aligns with their personal values. To demonstrate the effectiveness of this small modification, researchers told study participants about a proposal to increase the price of gas by 20 cents a gallon as a way of helping to reduce overall gas consumption. However, half the participants were told the policy was going to be implemented as soon as possible, and the other half were told that it would be implemented in four years. When the policy was expected to be put in place immediately, only 26 percent supported it, but when it was expected to lie dormant for four years before being officially implemented, many more people, over 40 percent in fact, were willing to support the gas price rise policy. A number of other experiments run by the same team of researchers showed a similar effect in other domains, such as charitable giving and health-related choices.

Behavioral economists have shown the effectiveness of this technique in another important domain: saving for the future. In one of the most powerful demonstrations of this persuasion strategy, *Nudge* co-author Richard Thaler and his research colleague Shlomo Benartzi showed that they could drastically boost participation rates in 401(k) plans. Using what they called the "Save More Tomorrow" program, rather than asking workers to participate in the program immediately, they instead asked workers to commit to putting a portion of their future salary increases into the plan. Although this program was successful for many reasons, one central reason is that it effectively shifted workers' thoughts about the program from the concrete terms associated with it (e.g., "I'll have less money in my paycheck each month") to more abstract terms about how it would help them achieve their broader values and goals (e.g., "I should do this because it's important and the right thing to do for my family").

The results of this research suggest that if you believe that you will encounter resistance with your requests for an immediate behavior change, you might be more successful if you instead ask your target to commit to the change at a given time in the future. For example, imagine you are a manager who has been charged with persuading employees to adopt a new system or procedure in your organization that will be beneficial to all concerned. Imagine further that, because previous attempts to install change in the organization haven't been as successful as had been hoped, you expect a struggle to get these plans implemented. One small difference in approach would be to get a head start by asking employees to agree to making the change in three months' time. Doing so would likely result in greater initial agreement to the new procedures as well as in increased future commitment, compared to just asking them to accept immediate change.

Another potential area for deploying future lock-ins is in subscriptions to common services such as Internet broadband, cable TV, and cellular phone plans. In order for customers to get the most attractive deals, suppliers often require them to be immediately locked in to a fixed-length contract of, say, 18 or 24 months. When learning about these instant lock-ins, some customers might object because they have focused on the immediate and concrete costs of the deal. However if that contractual lock-in was to occur three months after the beginning of the contract, it might not only reduce the overall number of customer objections, but also benefit the supplier by allowing them to keep each customer for an extra three months. And everybody wins, since the customers would have flexibility in that first three months to decide whether they were satisfied with the service.

Of course we recognize that in an ideal world it would be preferable not to have to wait at all. But sometimes, as we occasionally pointed out to our editors, a little late is certainly better than never.

## CHAPTER 15

# What SMALL BIG do you owe it to yourself to act on?

Every day we see persuasive messages appealing to our sense of obligation and moral responsibility to other people. Commercials tell us we owe it to our families to buy life insurance. Politicians tell us we owe it to our fellow citizens to buy products produced domestically. Environmentalists tell us we owe it to future generations to conserve the world's natural resources. And our conscience tells us we owe it to our parents to take care of them as they get older after all they've done for us. It's clear that we owe it to a lot of different people to do the right things in life, but is there one person out there whom we might owe it to the most?

How about your future self?

Researchers Christopher Bryan and Hal Hershfield explored the hypothesis that people can be persuaded to engage in behaviors that are beneficial to themselves in the long-term (even if they are seemingly costly in the short-term) by appealing to their sense of moral responsibility to the future version of themselves.

Considering that most people are in danger of not saving enough to ensure a financially secure future, the specific behavior that Bryan and Hershfield examined was saving money for retirement. To test their ideas, the researchers studied nearly

200 staff members of a university who had not been contributing much to their retirement plans.

All staff members enrolled in the study were sent a message reminding them of the importance of saving for retirement and strongly encouraging them to increase their savings rate. However, the last paragraph of the message differed significantly depending on which group the staff members were randomly assigned to.

For example, in the "standard future self-interest" condition, participants read, "We urge you to consider your long-term interests and to start saving more now. After all, your long-term well-being is at stake. Your decisions now will determine how much money is available to you when you retire."

In the "obligation to future self" condition, participants read, "We urge you to consider the responsibility you have to yourself in retirement and to start saving more now. After all, your 'future self' is completely dependent on you. Your decisions now will determine how much financial security your future self can count on."

Two weeks later, the researchers asked the university benefits office to report how much participants changed their retirement plan savings rate after they viewed the message. Those who received the "obligation to future self" message increased their savings rate by 0.85 percent more than those who received the "standard future self-interest" message. At first glance this doesn't seem that much of a difference, but consider the results if a 30-year-old man earning the national median salary of $45,485 per year increases his standard 5 percent contribution to 5.85 percent. Assuming he gets no raises over his lifetime (an extremely conservative estimate), on retirement at 65 years of age that small increase will have accrued an extra $68,797 of savings. Another way of looking at it is that the man in this example can retire roughly one and a half years earlier simply because of his response to the owe-it-to-yourself persuasive message!

This research demonstrates how appealing to people's moral responsibility to the future version of themselves can be a powerful influence strategy. However, it is important to note that the "obligation to future self" message didn't work for everyone. It turns out that people vary somewhat on how close they feel to their future selves. That is, the researchers found that those who felt little connection to their future selves were equally persuaded by both messages. Does this mean that when encouraging people to make financial plans for the future, you'll have to somehow identify those people who have a particular closeness to their future selves and segment your message accordingly? Actually, no. Although this strategy didn't work for everyone, the fact that the "obligation to future self" message fared no worse than the "standard future self-interest" message for those who didn't feel connected to their future selves suggests that the former strategy is probably the best overall strategy to employ.

The idea that big differences in retirement savings can result from the small act of asking people to consider their moral obligation to their future selves should appeal to financial advisers, HR managers, and policy makers alike. But is there an even more effective way to focus people's attention on the importance of considering their future selves? It turns out there is—show them a photo of what they likely will look like in the future.

In the studies, this time conducted by Hal Hershfield and six other researchers, participants first uploaded photographs of themselves a few weeks prior to the study. When the study started they were asked to indicate how much they would like to contribute to their retirement fund using an on-screen slider that controlled their level of contribution. Half entered their contributions on a screen that displayed the "current" photograph that the participant had uploaded. However, the other half saw an "age-progressed" photo portraying how they would likely look at the age of 70. This small change made a huge difference. Participants in the "future self" condition allocated an average of 6.2 percent of their earnings to their savings plan compared to an average of 4.4 percent by those in the "current self" condition. That's more than a 40 percent difference in savings driven by participants' contact with their future selves via the age-progressed photo.

The implications are clear. Any communicator challenged with changing the behaviors of someone who won't experience the benefit of those changes for a considerable time should not only point out the obligation they have to their future self but also illustrate what that future self will look like. For example, a doctor wishing to persuade a patient to give up smoking might run a photograph through a free age-progression app online to highlight how smoking can speed up aging.

But if the opportunity of providing an image of another's future self proves to be problematic, such as when seeking to persuade lots of people, additional research conducted by Daniel Bartels and Oleg Urminsky suggests an altogether easier approach. Their studies show that a communicator may be able to strengthen people's sense of connection between their current selves and their future selves by simply reminding them that even though some aspects of their lives will change over time, each person's core identity—who they really are as a person—will remain the same.

As a result, rather than just employing guilt strategies or complex incentive schemes to reduce, let's say, overeating or overspending, simply reminding people of their connectedness to their future selves may help them resist temptation and make more farsighted decisions.

You might think that the tactical shifts recommended in this chapter seem too small in scope to work. But, at the very minimum, you owe it to your future self to try out the new tactics and to see if they work for you.

## CHAPTER 16

# What SMALL BIG can reconnect people to their goals?

In 1919 Walt Disney was fired from his job drawing political cartoons for the *Kansas City Star* newspaper because, according to the paper's editor, "He wasn't creative enough."

In 2012, British biologist Sir John Gurdon's long and distinguished contribution to physiology and medicine was recognized with a Nobel Prize despite an Eton schoolmaster writing on his report card, "I believe Gurdon has ideas about becoming a scientist; based on his present showing this is quite ridiculous."

And according to Hollywood folklore, a studio manager at RKO Pictures was reputed to have written off Fred Astaire in an early screen test, saying, "[He] can't act. Can't sing. Balding. Can dance a little."

Happily, these early setbacks weren't enough to deter each from the goals they had set for themselves. Each went on to achieve amazing things. But sometimes people do get diverted and disengage from their goals—not the big, once-in-a-lifetime, dream factory kind of goals that future Nobel Prize winners and Hollywood icons will aspire to achieve, but smaller yet still important everyday goals, like saving a bit more money, losing some weight, paying off a credit card debt, or reaching this month's sales quota.

People often need to reengage with a previous goal they have set themselves. Similarly, managers, team supervisors, teachers, and even parents will sometimes need to reconnect and engage their staffs, students, and kids with an earlier objective, too. Traditionally when we set new goals either for ourselves or for others, the received wisdom has been to be very specific about what needs to be achieved. For example, lose two pounds a week, run six miles in 60 minutes, or save $100 every month for next year's vacation fund. But is this common wisdom really true when we're persuading ourselves or others to *reengage* with a goal?

Marketing professors Maura Scott and Stephen Nowlis thought that even though it makes intuitive sense for people to create a single, specific number goal for a new objective or endeavor, this may not necessarily be the case when it comes to reengaging with one's previous goals. Instead, they believed that people would be much more likely to reengage with prior goals if—rather than setting a single, specific number goal (e.g., lose 3 pounds a week)—they set a goal with a high-low range that averaged the same (e.g., lose 2–4 pounds a week).

To test their ideas the researchers set up a series of studies including one that took place in a weight loss club. Members who agreed to participate in the ten-week program first established their weight loss goals for the period and were then assigned to one of two weight loss groups—either a single-number goal group or a high-low range goal group. For example, members wishing to lose 2 pounds in the first week would be given the goal to "lose 2 pounds this week" if they were assigned to the single-number group or given the goal to "lose 1–3 pounds this week" if they were assigned to the high-low range number group.

At the beginning of each week participants would weigh in, establish their weight loss goal for the following week, and then take part in a group session in which they learned about healthy lifestyle practices. At the end of the ten-week period, the researchers measured both the dieters' performance—in terms of the amount of weight they lost—and willingness to reengage in another ten-week program. Although there wasn't much difference in terms of weight loss between the groups (during the first three weeks, those in the high-low range group lost an average 2.67 pounds compared to 2.2 pounds in the single-number goal group), the high-low range goal had a huge effect on persuading dieters to reengage and enroll in a further ten-week program. Just over 50 percent of those assigned a single-number weight loss goal enrolled in a future weight loss program, but close to 80 percent of those assigned a high-low range weight loss goal enrolled in further programs, paying a $25 fee to do so.

Diet club leaders and health club managers should take note. Even though the amount of weight lost across the two groups was similar, as any nutritionist will tell you, it is sustained weight loss over time that matters most. Given that a key ingredient to sustainability is helping people to reconnect to their goals over time, this could be one small change that you could make that would lead to a big difference. But why?

Previous research has shown that two factors can have an important influence on people when pursuing a goal: *challenge and attainability*. People should feel sufficiently challenged by a goal, because that will contribute to their feeling a sense of accomplishment, but only to the extent that there is a realistic possibility that the goal can be attained. Unlike single-number goals, wherein someone may have to pick a number that is relatively easily attainable, relatively challenging, or a compromise somewhere in between, high-low range goals have the advantage of engaging both these factors. In essence they influence goal reengagement by providing feelings of accomplishment driven by both the attainability and the challenge of the goal.

It is obvious that the subsequent success of Walt Disney, Fred Astaire, and Sir John Gurdon following their initial setbacks wasn't simply the result of doing something small, like changing the way they set goals for themselves. To become a Nobel Prize winner or a Hollywood icon requires huge sacrifices, hard work and study, and years of dedicated practice to nurture and develop talent. These are all BIG things.

But as we continually show throughout this book, small things matter too.

As this research clearly demonstrates, making a small change to the way we set our own and others' goals can make for BIG differences when it comes to engagement. A teacher, eager to reengage a pupil who recently performed poorly on a spelling bee, might set a high-low range goal of 7–9 correct words out of 10 on tomorrow's test rather than just aiming for a score of 8. A call center supervisor, keen to encourage and maintain high call volume levels, might experiment with single-number goals on one shift (for example, calling $x$ number of customers per day) and high-low range goals on another shift (for example, making $y$–$z$ number of calls per day) and then measure the differences this small change makes. Debt management companies and financial savings firms could find that repayment (and savings) plans are sustained much longer by their customers if they agree to high-low range repayment (savings) goals—for example, having customers pay back (save) $28–$32 a month rather than $30 a month.

A small change in the way people can be reconnected to their goals could have broader policy implications, too. Following a recommendation from the World Health Organization, a number of countries, including the United States of America, the United Kingdom, and Germany, have adopted 5 A Day programs that encourage citizens to consume five portions of fruit and vegetables each day. Many of these programs have measured only mixed success for a variety of reasons. This research suggests that making a small change to the 5 A Day stipulation (for example, making it 4–6 portions a day) could serve to reengage those who have aborted previous attempts to achieve the goal.

## CHAPTER 17

# What SMALL BIGs can be used to make defaults more effective?

E ven though we may not recognize it at the time, many of the choices that we make in our information-laden lives are essentially choices we have made without ever bothering to choose. Government policy makers, 401(k) savings plans, and car dealers alike all recognize the powerful draw of the "default" option and employ it to influence our behavior in some way or other.

For example, enrollments into tax-efficient 401(k) company savings plans can be as much as 50 percent higher if an employer sets a default automatic enrollment for employees as opposed to an active opt-in. An individual's willingness to carry an organ donation card can be four times higher in countries where consent to donate is automatically assumed unless citizens specifically opt out. Defaults are also extensively used by Internet marketers who will send you email offers and marketing messages unless you actively decline to receive them.

It is because default settings tend to work *with*, as opposed to *against*, our tendency toward inertia that they can be such a useful and efficient tool when it comes to influencing the decisions and behaviors of others. Why go to the trouble of asking people to think about changing when a small modification to the default setting can get them to change without their having to think at all? But, despite both their widespread appeal and ubiquitous presence, default options are not without their problems.

One downside is that defaults are typically passive rather than active, and as we have shown in previous chapters this can create problems when we want to persuade people to live up to their commitments in the future. Another challenge when using defaults is the fact that, because they are optimally employed in situations where there is a single best course of action, when we want people to consider several options before deciding, or at least tailor choices to their own individual needs, they don't work as well.

Is the answer, then, to ditch defaults in place of other more effective strategies? Certainly not. Rather fortunately, behavioral science offers up a couple of small changes that make it entirely possible to increase the effectiveness of a default strategy, without incurring any extra costs in terms of time and resources.

In a series of studies, researchers Punam Keller and colleagues showed that default strategies could be boosted by adopting a two-step approach that they call the "Enhanced Active Choice."

The first step of the Enhanced Active Choice approach requires a small change in the default setting so that, as opposed to opting in or opting out of one option, people are instead asked to make a real choice between two options. In one of their experiments Keller and her colleagues assigned employees of an educational facility to one of two groups. Participants in both groups were offered the chance to receive a flu shot that would not only protect their health, but also save them money on their monthly health insurance premiums.

The first group (the opt-in group) was simply asked to "Check the box if you would like to receive a flu shot this fall."

However, rather than defaulting the second group into a choice that had already been made for them, they were instead defaulted into making an active choice between two options. Specifically they were asked to check one of the following options:

I will get a flu shot this fall.

or

I will not get a flu shot this fall.

The results showed that many more people were willing to get a flu shot in the active choice condition (62 percent) than the opt-in condition (42 percent), providing solid evidence that while the opt-in strategy was reasonably successful, a small change that simply required people to make an active choice led to a much bigger difference.

But the researchers weren't finished. They also wondered how active choices could be enhanced further, and they found their answer in another fundamental principle of persuasion science: *loss aversion*—that is, the strong tendency in people to want to avoid losing or missing out. With this human tendency in mind, the researchers tested an enhancement to their active choice condition that pointed out what participants stood to lose if they failed to take action.

Specifically the participants of this group were asked to check one of these two options:

I will get a flu shot this fall to reduce my risk of getting the flu and I want to save $50.

or

I will not get a flu shot this fall even if it means I may increase my risk of getting the flu and I will not save $50.

The small act of accompanying an active choice with a specific loss message led to a big difference, with 75 percent of people indicating that they would now get the flu shot. Such impressive results led Keller and her colleagues to test similar approaches outside of their lab, including a large-scale field study of some 11,000 Pharmacy Benefit members. In each case their Enhanced Active Choice strategy was shown to be more effective.

Although these studies were conducted in a public health environment where the objective was to persuade people to sign up for a flu vaccination, the enhanced active choice approach should also be quite effective in other contexts. For example, rather than employing a standard default approach, software developers, keen to encourage users to move from a free, feature-limited version of their software to a fully functioning paid-for one, should change their pop-ups so users are required to actively choose between *two options*, remembering to enhance that active choice by pointing out what users stand to lose if they remain with the free version (e.g., they'd lose faster download times and extra features).

Financial institutions that wish to persuade customers to switch to alternative savings accounts might, when customers log in to online banking, present them with an active choice between their current account and an improved account, again being sure to point out what they are currently losing by not switching. School principals might persuade more parents to enroll their children in the weekly "walk to school" initiative by asking them to make an active choice between driving to school on a given day or walking—again being sure to point out the fresh air, extra exercise, and social inclusion that their kids could potentially miss if they choose not to walk.

Whatever the influence challenge, the key to activating this two-step approach is always the same. First take the small step to consider the two choices that you want your audience to actively choose from. Then take the *additional small step* to enhance your preferred choice by pointing out what could be lost if it is not selected.

These two small changes could lead to BIG differences in your success.

## CHAPTER 18

# What SMALL BIG can reduce people's tendency to procrastinate? (And yours too!)

In a recent set of annual accounts, the US retailer Best Buy reported a gain of over $40 million from customers who had failed to redeem gift cards before the expiration date. It appears that it's not an isolated phenomenon. The Tower Group, a consumer research company, estimates that the total value of money that goes unused on gift cards by the time expiration dates are reached is close to $2 billion annually.

Learning of these huge surpluses of unused cash, some consumer groups have called for a change to the law requiring retailers to further extend the expiration dates on the gift cards they issue in an effort to give people more time to redeem them. But based on what we know from research into the persuasion process, this kind of a change, rather than improve matters, is likely to make matters much worse. We believe that an entirely different approach is needed. In fact, it is an approach that requires the deployment of just a small change that engages a central motivation to act. Deploying this costless small change may not only increase the probability that your cousin will use that $25 Amazon.com gift certificate you purchased for him last holiday, but it could also help you persuade someone not to put off until tomorrow what they really should be doing today.

We all know that there are occasions when we procrastinate.

Whether it's exercising a little more, starting that new study assignment, or mowing the lawn, many of us can display remarkable inventiveness when it comes to stalling for time. As the Spanish proverb states, "Tomorrow is always the busiest day of the week." Typically procrastination is associated with tasks that people find less pleasant to carry out, but it turns out that oftentimes we are just as likely to put off until tomorrow activities that we actually find fun and enjoyable. Why?

One reason is that, because people are so focused on dealing with whatever is vying for their attention at a specific moment in time, they wrongly believe that once they have gotten that albatross off their back they will have more time in the future to carry out more enjoyable activities. Of course what they fail to realize is that that albatross was one of a flock and another one will invariably take its place, meaning that they will be just as busy in the future and, as a result, simply end up not completing even enjoyable activities.

Noting that in a busy information-overloaded world people are increasingly as likely to procrastinate desirable tasks as undesirable ones, researchers Suzanne Shu and Ayelet Gneezy set up a fascinating series of experiments. In doing so they uncovered how a small change to the expiration date can have a remarkable and counter-intuitive effect on people's likelihood to complete a task.

Before the studies got going the researchers asked people to rate the attractiveness of a gift certificate that was good for coffee and cake worth $6 at a high-quality local bakery store. They were also asked the likelihood that they would redeem it should they be given one. Unbeknownst to the participants, although the gift certificates they reviewed were equal in terms of their cash value, they were different in terms of their expiration date: One was valid for just three weeks, but the other was good for two months. There was no doubt that when people were asked to evaluate the certificates, those with the longer expiration date received much more positive feelings than those with the shorter ones.

Interestingly, it appears that this positive evaluation influenced their predictions of whether they would use the certificate too. Close to 70 percent of those who evaluated the certificate with the two-month expiration period said they would use it, compared to roughly 50 percent who evaluated the three-week expiration period certificate. Clearly people appear to like the greater flexibility that a longer expiration date offers. Recall how in the introduction to this book we offered evidence of how poorly people predict their future behaviors. Could it be that even though people prefer the gift certificate with the longer expiration date they would, in fact, be more likely to use the gift certificate with the shorter one?

That's exactly what the researchers set out to test and what they found was astonishing. Despite participants' predictions to the contrary, five times as many given the short-expiration date certificate visited the bakery to claim their coffee and cake than those given the long-expiration date certificates. People may have preferred the offer with a longer expiration date because it afforded them more time to redeem the offer; however, in reality, it actually caused fewer of them to do so.

As a final check to ensure that the results of the study were attributable principally to procrastination and not to other factors, the researchers completed a series of follow-up surveys. Those who did redeem the certificates reported an enjoyable and worthwhile experience. Those who didn't conveyed their regret and were most likely to agree with statements such as "I got too busy and ran out of time" or "I kept thinking that I would do it a bit later" as opposed to other explanations such as "I forgot," "I don't like pastries," or "It seemed like too much effort."

The result of this research suggests an immediate small change that any communicator can make when seeking to persuade clients or customers to take up offers and proposals. Instead of offering a longer time frame in order for your target audience to respond, in the mistaken belief that doing so will make it more attractive, this research suggests that a much shorter time frame should be offered. For example, a software company seeking to boost new-user registrations might see improvements if their pop-up box is changed from the standard options "Register now," "Ask again tomorrow," and "Ask again next week" to "Register now," "Ask again tomorrow," and "Remind me again in 3 days (last day to register)," perhaps offering additional benefits or bonuses to encourage early registrations.

A financial adviser or investment manager, seeking to persuade potential investors to attend a webinar or presentation on the latest investment tips, may increase sign-up rates by changing the "RSVP by" date on the invitation to one that looms sooner, rather than later. This is consistent with other research showing that email invitations indicating a specific and close deadline increase click-through registration rates by 8 percentage points.

Finally, if your spouse, friend, or business partner has promised to share a fine and presumably delicious wine with you but keeps putting it off while waiting for a special enough occasion, Shu and Gneezy would point you to a scene from the hit movie *Sideways* for a clue for how to potentially persuade him or her:

**Miles:** I've got a couple things I'm saving. I guess the star would be a 1961 Cheval Blanc.

**Maya:** You've got a '61 Cheval Blanc that's just sitting there?…It might be too late already. What are you waiting for?

**Miles:** I don't know. Special occasion. With the right person. It was supposed to be for my tenth wedding anniversary.

**Maya:** The day you open a '61 Cheval Blanc, that's the special occasion.

## CHAPTER 19

# What SMALL BIG can keep your customers hooked?

In a 1981 hit that appeared in VH1's Top 100 Greatest Hard Rock Songs, the UK punk rock band The Clash asked, "Should I stay or should I go?" The question posed in their song is likely to be asked as often today as it was upon its release 30 years ago—and not just pertaining to matters of the heart, but to matters of business, too.

Every day millions of customers ask themselves, "Should I stay or should I go?" when finding themselves waiting in line for a service and not knowing how long their wait is likely to be. Shoppers may switch from one line to another in checkouts hoping to pick a faster-moving one. Web users might refresh their browsers in the hope that a chosen download will run faster. Customers contacting a telephone helpline may abandon a current call and call back later in the hope that the wait time will be shorter. We might be living in the fastest-moving, most information-saturated environment ever, but we still spend a considerable amount of our time waiting in line (or online).

Noting that the average American citizen can spend upwards of two years of his or her life waiting in line, researchers Narayan Janakiraman, Robert Meyer, and Stephen Hoch sought to identify the factors that will typically persuade people to stay in line, and what will convince them to abandon the wait completely. Their findings point to several small but important changes that any business or customer service organization can make that could lead to big improvements in customer retention, satisfaction, and service scores.

At the core of this research is the simple intuition that "a queue worth joining is a queue worth persisting in" is advice that is rarely taken. For example, studies have found that as many as a third of callers who are held in line when they contact a call center will hang up and dial again primarily as a result of pure impatience. Tellingly, few people ever benefit from such a strategy because they typically call back at some time in the future and their total cumulative wait time becomes much longer.

When viewed through the lens of persuasion science, deciding "Should I stay or should I go?" pits two fundamental human motivations against each other. On one hand the longer people wait in a queue, the more likely they are to focus their attention on alternative activities they could be accomplishing instead of waiting. Not attending to these alternative activities could be viewed as a "loss" and—given that a fundamental motivation that we all have is to avoid losing—people waiting in line might be motivated to abandon the wait simply to avoid any further loss.

However things are rarely as straightforward as they seem. A case could also be made that people who join a queue have made an active commitment, and therefore the principle of consistency might be activated, causing them to stay put. As each minute of waiting time passes it is possible that their motivation to stay in line actually increases the closer they get to their goal.

So in the context of this tension between avoiding loss and maintaining consistency, what do people typically do? In their studies Janakiraman and his colleagues find that most people make arguably the worst decision of all by abandoning their waits somewhere in the middle. No doubt that this less-than-optimal decision will likely be accompanied by feelings of annoyance, frustration, and displeasure—hardly a desirable situation if the company that these potential customers are waiting to do business with is your company.

This prompts a question: What can be done to mitigate these feelings and to reduce the number of customers who hang up before speaking with your organization? Some obvious answers would be to hire and train more phone staff or to reduce call wait times by analyzing demand and capacity and then managing it more efficiently. While all important, these seem like pretty big and costly endeavors. Given that this book is primarily concerned with deploying the smallest and least resource-intensive strategies, what else could be done? In their studies, which included several laboratory experiments as well as field data from a call center in India, Janakiraman and his colleagues tested an easily implemented small BIG that showed good results: Simply providing those in line with distractions and other basic activities for them to engage in while waiting led to a significant reduction in dropped calls. Sounds fairly straightforward, but it works.

We wonder whether this might also provide one of those opportunities in business to turn what is a largely frustrating experience for most people into a positive, and to even create future loyalty. Financial institutions could provide customers waiting on phones with simple tips on money management via their automated voice system or, for customers in bank offices, with activities for kids to teach them about money. A restaurant hostess, rather than leaving those placemats that double as coloring activities for children on the tables, might hand them out to families that are waiting in line to be seated. Embassies experiencing long lines of visa applicants could provide useful distractions for people in the form of information sheets containing common phrases, translations, and insights on local customs such as tipping (or queuing!) that they will find helpful when they arrive.

On the subject of distractions we are reminded of two wonderful examples. The first was related to us by a reader of our INSIDE INFLUENCE blog who recounted a story of a customer who, on calling his cell phone provider, was told by the customer service agent that her system was running slow and in order to save him from waiting, she would call him back later. Having already waited some time to get through, this customer wasn't going to give up the connection so easily and instead insisted that he stay on the line and wait. "Very well Sir," replied the customer service agent, "if that's the case then perhaps you would tell me your favorite song." The customer was completely puzzled by such a random question but answered anyway. Imagine his sheer astonishment when, having replied "'New York, New York' by Frank Sinatra," the customer service agent began singing it to him.

The second example comes from our UK editor who told us that after calling the Cats Protection Agency he was put on hold, but rather than hearing music, he instead heard the soothing sounds of cats purring.

So maybe the small BIG here is for companies to allow people to personalize their choice of on-hold music while waiting. Our choice?

The Clash of course!

## CHAPTER 20

# What is the SMALL BIG that could turn your potential into reality?

Suppose that you are looking to persuade a new client that yours is the company that deserves a lucrative contract. Alternatively, imagine you want to position yourself as the obvious choice for a new job or promotion. Will you be more successful by making small changes in your approach to highlight your previous experiences and past successes? Or would you be better advised to focus on your potential instead, pointing out to the client or recruiter what you can deliver in the future?

In a quick (and admittedly very unscientific) survey that one of us conducted with folks in the office, a clear answer to this question emerged. You should focus on your past experience and achievements. At first glance this seems to make sense. Actual and real achievements are surely more compelling than the potential to achieve in the future for good reason: They *have* already been accomplished. They are concrete. They leave no room for doubt. Therefore all other things being equal, when it comes to choosing which company will secure that lucrative new contract, the odds will surely favor the one with years of experience and a glut of industry awards compared to the less experienced new-kid-on-the-block that merely has the potential to do well. Similarly, the more attractive prospect for that promotion will be the candidate who has already achieved notable career success, not necessarily the candidate who merely has the potential to succeed.

But in reality this isn't always the case. Examples abound of budding sports stars who negotiate eye-popping sums of money on the basis of their future potential. Former NFL quarterback JaMarcus Russell was the first overall pick in the 2007 NFL draft, landing a contract with the Oakland Raiders worth an astounding $61 million. Clearly the Raiders saw such potential in Russell that they were persuaded to pay top dollar for his services—potential that never translated into on-field success. In the business world many of us can recall instances when the promising but inexperienced candidate landed the promotion over the more experienced colleague. And if you have ever worked in a business development or sales role, you will at some time have lost a deal to a competitor who, at least on paper, didn't come close to your levels of experience and past accomplishments.

So when it comes to persuading others, which should you focus on: *potential* or *reality*?

According to persuasion scientists Zakary Tormala, Jayson Jia, and Michael Norton (co-author of the excellent book *Happy Money*) you should focus on your potential because—somewhat counter-intuitively—the potential to be great at something will often seem more compelling to decision makers than actually being great at that very same thing. In other words, the promise of potential often outshines the reality.

In one of their studies Tormala and his colleagues asked participants to evaluate an applicant who had applied for a senior position in the banking division of a large company. All participants learned that the applicant had received his bachelor's degree from Cornell University, majored in economics with a 3.82 grade point average, and earned a master of business administration degree from New York University. However, some participants learned that the applicant had two years of relevant banking experience and had recently received a score of 92/100 on a test called the Assessment of Leadership Achievement, whereas other participants learned that the applicant had no relevant banking experience and had recently received a score of 92/100 on a test called the Assessment of Leadership Potential. All the participants were told that both tests assessed how a candidate would likely perform two years down the line.

Remarkably, the participants believed that the applicant in the *potential condition* would be a more successful hire than the applicant in the achievement condition. This was despite the fact that the applicant was objectively much less qualified due to having no prior relevant experience. Interestingly, when asked to predict which of the applicants they believed would be performing better after five years, participants were still much more likely to select the applicant in the potential condition achievement. In a follow-up study, Tormala and colleagues found the same results when participants had to choose between two individuals who differed on potential vs. actual achievement but who were comparable in every other way. These results clearly speak to the power of potential.

It turns out that the persuasive pull of potential over reality didn't just hold true in a recruitment setting. Tormala and his colleagues also found evidence for the *preference for potential* effect in a more consumer-based environment among users of a social media website. In the study, Facebook users were shown a series of quotes about a comedian. Half were shown comments highlighting the comedian's potential such as "This guy could become the next big thing" and "Next year everyone could be talking about this comedian." The other half were shown comments that focused attention on the comedian's actual achievements like, "Critics say he has become the next big thing" and "Everyone is talking about this guy."

As was the case with the banking recruitment study, and further demonstrating a general preference for potential over accomplishment, Facebook users registered much greater interest (measured by click rates) and liking (measured by fan rates) when quotes about the comedian's potential, rather than actual achievements, were highlighted.

But why?

The researchers believe that one potential* reason why potential will often capture attention more than reality is due to the fact that reality has happened, making it completely certain. Whereas despite the obvious disadvantages that potential can inject into a message or a communication, the uncertainty that the audience experiences when evaluating the person with potential serves to offer a wonderful advantage—namely, a tendency to arouse more interest.

So does this mean that when it comes to decision making, people will believe potential to be a more reliable decision trigger than reality? Hardly. But given that potential has an arousing quality, which in turn can persuade people to pay greater attention, it makes sense for any communicator to align appeals in a way that prospers from this insight. In fact, the authors of the study go on to make this exact point, suggesting that if supporting information is provided immediately after attention is focused on potential (e.g., a testimonial from a trusted source, a high leadership score, or some other type of persuasive message), the likelihood of a favorable attitude or impression is increased.

Suppose then that the time has come to make the case to a prospective client that yours is the company to do business with. Suppose further that you believe a competitive advantage that your company provides is a mixture of relevant previous

---

*We're sorry.

experience coupled with new ways of thinking. One small but important area you should pay careful attention to is the order in which you present that combination of advantages. You should position your messages in a way that first focuses that client's attention on the potential future benefits that your proposal offers, followed by examples of what your organization has previously delivered.

Similarly if you are applying for a promotion, or providing an endorsement for someone who is, then these studies suggest that you would be more effective by first highlighting the future potential you (or the person you are recommending) will bring to the role rather than immediately leading with your prior experience. Doing so could increase the chances that you will capture a recruiter's interest, meaning that the subsequent information you convey about actual achievements and experience will get more focused attention. Similarly, high school graduates should alert college admissions officers to the potential they offer early on in the personal statements that accompany their college applications.

Real estate agents looking to market an undesirable property might create a more favorable image in prospective buyers' minds by making small changes that focus more on a property's potential. For example, they could highlight the possibilities that exist for turning that run-down building into a home office or a delightful retreat for your favorite mother-in-law or suggest that you could "realize your dreams with this renovation project."

Emphasizing one's potential could also prove valuable for jobseekers who find themselves with a resume that contains less work experience than likely rival candidates. Here the recommendation is not to focus on one's experience but instead to focus on upside evidence. Will this simple shift alone be enough to get the job? Maybe not, but it could at least be the key that unlatches the door to a meeting where many other small BIG insights from this book could then be deployed to make a good result more likely.

## CHAPTER 21

# What SMALL BIGs could help you lead more productive meetings?

If there's any truth in the saying "Meetings are where minutes are taken and hours are wasted," then there is a fair chance that you have come away from a few meetings wondering if anything productive has been accomplished. Over 25 years ago psychologists Garold Stasser and William Titus published their seminal work on how people communicate in decision-making groups. Yet despite these studies being a quarter of a century old, for many the results remain just as relevant today.

They found that a significant amount of time in meetings was typically spent listening to people telling each other what everyone else already knew. Perhaps even more distressing was the discovery that those individuals attending meetings who actually possessed genuinely new information—information that only they knew about—often failed to alert the rest of the group to this new information.

The result: decisions that were at best okay, and at worst pretty poor.

More recent studies have confirmed these findings. Take, by way of an example, a study conducted by James Larson Jr. and colleagues in which a number of doctors were shown videos of two specific medical cases. The doctors were split into small groups to see the videos but, unbeknownst to them, each group watched a slightly different video. Additionally, some doctors were provided with individual information about each of the cases. As a result, all the doctors received *some* relevant information about the two patient scenarios, but no one doctor received *all* the relevant information.

After watching the videos the doctors were asked to discuss the two cases with one of the other groups and come to a consensus about both the diagnosis and the required treatments. Cleverly the researchers made sure that the most accurate diagnosis and treatment decisions could only be made if *all* the doctors contributed their respective knowledge to the group. What they found, though, was that the sharing and pooling of information rarely happened to the extent necessary for the most accurate diagnosis. As a result, less-than-optimal decision making led to poorer treatment decisions. In short, not a good outcome.

So what can be done to ensure that information is offered freely and communicated effectively? Here are four ways that you can small BIG your meetings both at work and at home.

The first small change that can make a big difference is to ask those attending to submit information *before* the meeting. This may sound somewhat obvious, but its practice is the exception rather than the rule. Making this small change can lead to contributions that are less likely to be influenced by those of others. It can be especially effective for meetings where a desired output is new ideas: Asking for contributions in advance often increases the number of voices that are heard, potentially leading to a greater number of ideas generated. It turns out that a similar approach can be applied to training sessions and family meetings too. For example, when facing a situation or challenge that would benefit from the collective input of every member of the group, instead of asking everyone to submit their ideas and suggestions at the same time, it can be much more effective to ask people to spend a few moments quietly reflecting on their ideas, writing them down, and in turn submitting them to the group. Doing this can help ensure that any potentially insightful ideas from quieter members of the group don't get crowded out by members with louder voices. The small change required here costs nothing more than a couple moments of silence.

A second small change that can make for big differences is to make sure that the person who leads the meeting always speaks *last*. It is remarkable how common it is for people who lead meetings to fail to notice their influence over the group. If a leader, manager, or a family elder contributes an idea first, group members will often unwittingly follow suit, leading to alternative ideas and insights being lost. One way to avoid this potentially unhelpful influence is to ensure that the leader solicits the opinions and inputs of others *before* publicly declaring his or her own.

Third, it can be helpful to recognize the value of a checklist. One way that physicians now routinely ensure that they avoid making less-than-optimal decisions and collectively take the right course of action is to make use of a simple checklist. As Atul Gawande recounts in his book *The Checklist Manifesto*, these lists contain some surprisingly obvious but disastrous-if-missed items. Is this the right patient? Do I have their medical records? Are they allergic to anything? Do I know their blood type?

Much like a pilot will employ a checklist as part of their preflight activity, there is a lot to be said for the organizer of a meeting to consider the essential items that should appear on their pre-meeting checklist. Are the right people in attendance? Is the balance of expertise correct? Is someone coming who will dissent in a positive way?

Finally, recent research by Juliet Zhu and J. J. Argo suggests that making subtle changes to the seating arrangements in meetings can have an effect on what people choose to focus their attention on. For example, the study found that circular seating arrangements typically activated people's need to belong. As a result they were more likely to focus on the group's collective objectives and be persuaded by messages and proposals that highlighted group benefits rather than benefits to any one individual. This effect was reversed, however, when the seating arrangement was either angular (think L-shaped) or square. These seating arrangements tended to activate people's need for uniqueness. As a result, people were more responsive and reacted more favorably to messages and proposals that were self-oriented and that allowed them to elevate their individualism.

The researchers concluded that if the goal of your meeting is to create an atmosphere of collaboration and cooperation between people, seating arrangements that are circular will likely be more conducive. Therefore a team leader whose challenge is to persuade staff to generate next steps and future actions that will be contingent on people working together would be advised to ensure that a circular seating arrangement is arranged. This might be especially important should they have a member of the staff that has a reputation for marginalizing themselves.

However, if the team leader's goal is to focus their staff's attention on taking responsibililty for more individual actions, then an angular seating arrangement, such as square or rectangular, might be a better alternative.

Of course in some instances the meetings you arrange may require elements of both colloborative *and* individual working. As a result, it might be neccesary for you to arrange for seating arrangements to be changed during the meeting. For example, a conference organizer recognizing the need for cooperation and joint work during the early stages of a meeting should arrange for people to be seated in a circular fashion during that time and, where neccesary, make a small change to create angular seating arrangements when the focus of the meeting shifts to topics that require individual attention and focus. Another small change that the meeting's planner can adopt is to assign people to specific seats at tables rather than allowing people to select their own (remember, birds of a feather invariably flock together). As any wedding planner will tell you, people are remarkably compliant when they see their name on a place card.

# CHAPTER 22

# What SMALL BIG could ensure you are dressed for success?

It's taken you weeks, perhaps even months, of hard work and tenacity, but it appears that your efforts are at last starting to pay dividends. Your phone rings. It's the personal assistant of that important and potentially lucrative new client you have been targeting. They are calling to confirm a meeting the following week. You briefly allow yourself a moment of self-congratulation before turning your attention to planning for the appointment. Meetings like this are hard to come by and the chances are you'll only have one opportunity to make a great impression. You want to come across as a trustworthy and credible communicator. Friendly, likeable, approachable, and influential.

So what exactly should you wear?

For many years persuasion scientists have been studying the effects of clothing on people's likelihood to be influenced. Social psychologist Leonard Bickman is perhaps best known for his studies demonstrating the powerful sway of the well-attired. Many of his experiments involved a researcher stopping passersby and asking them to comply with a request of some sort. Sometimes the request would be to pick up a piece of discarded litter, or to stand on a specific spot by a bus stop, or even—and this is our personal favorite—asking passersby to give coins for a car parking meter to a complete stranger.

In each case the small change that Bickman would make would be to vary not the requester, but simply what the requester was wearing. Sometimes the requester would be dressed in casual clothes and sometimes in a uniform such as that of a security guard. Tellingly, in surveys conducted prior to the studies, most participants would dramatically underestimate the influence that a uniformed requester would have on people's decisions to comply. But the results, of course, told a different story, with often *twice* as many people being persuaded to act when the requester wore the security guard uniform.

Other more recent studies have found similar effects. For example, a UK study demonstrated that people were significantly more likely to recall health messages given to them by a healthcare professional when that messenger was wearing a stethoscope than when no stethoscope was present. Interestingly the stethoscope never had to be used. In addition to acting as an effective tool to help medical professionals diagnose a potential condition, the stethoscope also acted as an effective tool to inform the patient of the wearer's credibility and knowledge.

Studies have shown that donning a straightforward business suit can have an equally persuasive effect. In one experiment, 350 percent more people were willing to follow a man crossing the street against a red light and against the traffic (and, incidentally, against the law) when he wore a suit rather than just casual clothes.

It is interesting to note that in all these studies, and others like them, a person's clothing was primarily influencing behavior for one very simple reason: No other information existed about the requester's expertise. The immediate implications are clear. When meeting someone for the first time it is important to dress at a level that matches one's true expertise and credentials. To do so is entirely in keeping with a fundamental principle of persuasion science—authority. Authority is the principle that influences people, especially when they are uncertain, to follow the advice and recommendations of those they perceive to have greater knowledge and trustworthiness.

But modern-day business meetings are rarely so straightforward. With the advent of different dress codes, from business formal to dress-down casual and a myriad others in between, perhaps it would be more effective to draw on another powerful driver of human decision making—*similarities.*

In previous chapters we have described how one potential route to effective persuasion for a communicator is to reach out by highlighting genuine commonalities that exist with audience members. What better way of highlighting similarities and minimizing dissimilarities than to find out the dress code of the specific organization and then match it on the day of your meeting? But, again, such an approach is not without its pitfalls. What if the dress code is one that you would not normally choose for yourself? Are you demonstrating true authenticity by matching their standard? And even if you are, could the upside of a similarity be a downside in that your authority and credibility could potentially be undermined?

Put more simply, is there a clear answer to the question, What is most persuasive—authority or similarity?

Unfortunately, we aren't aware of any research that directly answers this question. However, as is sometimes the case in persuasion, we would surmise that a more effective route might be to employ elements of both approaches. This could mean that, where and when it is appropriate, one might dress in a style similar to that of the person or group you wish to influence—but do so at one level higher. That could mean a neck tie or perhaps a jacket, for example, in an office that generally practices a more relaxed or casual dress policy.

## CHAPTER 23

## What SMALL change can have a BIG impact when it comes to positioning your team as experts?

U sually, a communicator's purpose is to develop and send a message that alters the attitudes, decisions, or behaviors of its recipients. The critical question, of course, is how best to arrange it.

Although social psychologists have provided many important insights into this matter over the years, one of the most valuable is offered by Anthony Greenwald in his "cognitive response model," which represents a subtle but critical shift in thinking about persuasion. According to Greenwald's model, the best indication of how much change a communication will produce lies *not* in what the communication itself says but, rather, in what the recipient of the communication will likely say to himself or herself as a result of receiving it.

When identifying the changes that can be made to a message that will lead to the biggest differences in its persuasiveness, researchers have traditionally focused on elements such as message clarity, structure, logic, and so on because it was thought that the recipient's comprehension of the message's content was critical to persuasion. Although this is certainly true, the cognitive response model adds an important insight by suggesting that the message itself is not directly responsible for change. Instead, the direct cause of any change is the result of another factor: Self-talk, the internal cognitive responses that people engage in after being exposed to a message. Or put more simply, what a person says to themselves after receiving a message.

A good deal of research supports the model. For instance, in one of Anthony Greenwald's persuasion experiments, audience members' attitude change on a topic wasn't related so much to what they recalled about the elements of the persuasive appeal as it was to what they recalled about the comments they'd made at the time.

So what might be the implications of this view when the time comes for you to fashion a persuasive attempt of your own? Suppose for a moment that you want to write a letter to the citizens of your town supporting lower highway speed limits. The most obvious implication is that you would be foolish to make this attempt without simultaneously thinking about what your audience members would say to themselves in response to the letter.

So what small steps could lead to big differences in the effectiveness of your communication? First, you should consider ways to stimulate readers to talk positively to themselves about all aspects of your letter. This means that in addition to considering the key features of your intended message (for example, the strength and logic of the arguments), you should also take into account an entirely different set of factors that are likely to spur positive responses. For instance, you may want to delay the mailing of your letter until your local newspaper reports a rash of highway accidents; that way, when your letter arrives, its message will gain validity with its recipients because of its good fit with other information. Or you might want to increase the favorable responses to your letter by printing it professionally on high quality paper because people will make the assumption that the more care and expense a communicator has put into a persuasion campaign, the more the communicator believes in its validity.

But, even more important than trying to ensure that your
message creates positive self-talk, another small but important
step that you should also think about is how to avoid negative
self-talk—especially in the form of internal counter-arguments
to your stated position.

Persuasion researchers have routinely shown that the
counter-arguments that audience members make in response to
a message can devastate its effectiveness. Thus, you might want
to include in your letter a quote from an acknowledged traffic
safety expert asserting that higher speed limits greatly increase
automobile fatalities.

Recent brain-imaging studies conducted by Jan Engelmann,
Monica Capra, Charles Noussair, and Gregory Berns tell us
why such a step would work. Participants in the study were
asked to make a series of unfamiliar financial choices, some
of which were accompanied by advice from an expert source
(a prominent economist). When the economist's guidance was
available, the participants' choices were powerfully affected by
this expert's advice. The reason was revealed in the brain acti-
vation patterns of the participants. In the presence of expert
advice, the areas of the participants' brains linked to critical
thinking and counter-arguing practically flatlined.

These findings help explain why expert communicators are
so effective. It's not that people look upon a legitimate authority's position merely as a single important factor that—when
combined with other important factors—tips the balance
in favor of one choice over another. Instead, and especially
when they are unsure of themselves, people allow the authority's opinion to dominate all the other factors—indeed, even
shutting down cognitive consideration of those other factors.
As one of the study's authors said in describing how his findings
challenged the traditional model of rational decision making,
"In this [traditional] worldview, people take advice, integrate it

with their own information, and come to a decision. If that were actually true, we'd have seen activity in brain regions that guide decisions. But, what we found is that when someone receives expert advice, that activity went away."

Two lessons emerge, both of which require a communicator's attention when structuring an influence attempt. First, because people frequently disengage their critical thinking and counter-arguing powers and defer to expert advice, communicators who can lay claim to relevant expertise would be foolish not to make that expertise known early in the process. In addition, steps should be taken to make clear the relevant credentials of the other members of your organization with whom audience members may be interacting. Although simple, it's surprising how often otherwise savvy communicators forget to credentialize themselves and their colleagues before an influence attempt is launched.

But when they do remember, the results can be impressive.

Take as an example a problem that blights a large number of health centers—too much demand for services and seemingly not enough capacity to meet this demand. When faced with such issues the immediate and obvious response is to simply increase capacity. However, not only is such a response very costly, but as many service organizations will attest, demand for services has a knack of expanding to fill any subsequent increases made in capacity. Newly qualified doctors in the UK, as with many of their colleagues around the world, will complete rotations in various hospitals and health centers after graduation. These rotations provide a significant boost to capacity in the centers; however, patients often appear reluctant to consult with these less experienced doctors, preferring instead to wait and see a resident doctor. But here's the rub. Given that they have recently graduated from some of the top medical schools in the country and come armed with the latest and most up-to-date skills and knowledge, it could be argued that an appointment with one of them would be a good choice for patients to make. There may be lots of demand in the health system, but often there is underutilized capacity, too. To redress this balance, a number of centers in the trials experimented by prominently highlighting the credentials and up-to-date knowledge of these doctors, usually accompanied by their photograph. Reception staff played a role too, by changing the all-too-common retort, "I can fit you in to see the locum doctor" (the medical equivalent of seeing a substitute teacher), with a credibility-enhancing "I can get you in to see our new highly qualified doctor who has joined us from the University Medical School." These small, and relatively cheap, interventions led to a dramatic reshaping of demand and capacity. Waiting times for appointments in some centers declined, often by as much as 50 percent, not due to a big system change but because of a small contextual one instead.

In addition to projecting your own and your team members' expert standing into the consciousness of an audience, it is equally important to protect that status by conveying your background, experience, and skills honestly without exaggeration. That is, if we overstate our know-how and are later discovered to have been deceptive in this regard, we will likely lose the ability to promote our expertise convincingly in the future, even along those dimensions where we can fairly claim it.

# What unexpected SMALL BIG can empower an uncertain expert?

In the last chapter we discussed how communicators, by high-lighting their expertise before presenting their message or proposal, can often register big differences in the subsequent response to those messages and proposals. Over two thousand years ago, the Roman poet Virgil advised that people should "believe an expert" and, as Jan Engelmann and his colleagues demonstrated in their brain-imaging studies, that advice remains just as relevant today. In fact a case could be made that Virgil's advice is even more relevant. Every day we face an onslaught of information, in our professional and personal lives, that we are required to navigate. In the context of such information overload, we search for decision-making shortcuts such as those provided by expert opinions. So, it is easy to see why those who have superior knowledge and wisdom can exert so much influence over our decision making.

Fortunately, there appears to be no shortage of experts willing to help. The business world provides a good illustration with a seemingly never-ending supply of specialists eager to aid any organization to make the right choices. The same is true in our personal lives. Financial advisers stand at the ready, armed with the latest investment advice, as do parental coaches with state-of-the-art child-rearing techniques, and personal trainers with cutting-edge advice on how to stay fit and healthy.

There is an irony here, though. Today's information-overloaded world requires us to look to experts to help guide our way, *but* there is also an overload of experts, all claiming that theirs is the advice we should listen to and follow. In this information-saturated world where so many claim to be an expert, how do we know who to follow?

Perhaps we should listen to the experts who sound the most confident. After all, we intuitively know that people are more often convinced by those experts who sound certain, right?

Actually, perhaps not!

Consumer researchers Uma Karmarkar and Zakary Tormala believe that it isn't always the recommendations and advice that emanate from the most confident-sounding expert that will carry sway. Instead, their studies find that often it is the advice and recommendations that come from experts who are themselves uncertain that is the most compelling. This is especially the case when advice concerns situations for which there is no one clear or obvious answer.

In one of Karmarkar and Tormala's studies, customers were shown a positive review for a new restaurant called Bianco's. Half of the customers were told that the review was written by a well-known and regularly published food critic, but the other half were told the review was written by a little-known blogger who mostly ate in fast-food restaurants. As you would expect, and consistent with lots of previous research, those who read the review written by the well-known and experienced restaurant reviewer were more influenced by the review than those who read the one written by an unknown blogger. But the researchers weren't finished.

As well as varying the expertise of each reviewer, they also varied how confident the reviewer felt about the review.

For example in a high-certainty condition the reviewer wrote, "I ate dinner there and can confidently give this restaurant a 4 star rating."

However in the low-certainty condition the reviewer wrote, "Because I have only eaten at Bianco's once I am not completely confident in my opinion but, for now, I am awarding this restaurant 4 stars."

Those folks who read the review from the expert who expressed uncertainty were significantly more favorable to the restaurant and rated the likelihood they would frequent it as much higher than those that read the reviews by the highly certain expert or the unknown blogger. In each case the review itself never changed—only the small degree of how confident the expert reviewer was.

In explaining their findings Karmarkar and Tormala point out that because people generally expect experts to be certain about their opinions, it's when an expert signals potential uncertainties that people are drawn in to what they are saying. In effect, the source's expertise, when coupled with a level of uncertainty, arouses *intrigue*. As a result, and assuming that the arguments that the expert makes are still reasonably strong, this *drawing in* of an audience to the features of the message can actually lead to more effective persuasion.

This insight offers an important lesson for communicators wishing to increase the persuasiveness of a message. It can be easy to conceal a small doubt, tiny niggle, or slight uncertainty in your argument, believing those small things could make a large and detrimental difference to your success. However, in situations where it is clear that no single obvious answer exists, signaling a small uncertainty, rather than being detrimental to your cause, could make a big and beneficial difference to it. As a result, when seeking to persuade decision makers, a business consultant, rather than hiding or covering up minor uncertainties about a recommendation, might instead embrace them in the knowledge that they can actually make him or her more persuasive—assuming, of course, that the case is a strong one. Doing so affords another advantage—it is a strategy that is likely to build trust as well.

## CHAPTER 25

# What SMALL BIG can prevent you from becoming the *Weakest Link*?

Since first appearing on TV, the quiz show the *Weakest Link* rose rapidly to become a worldwide success, being broadcast on TV screens in dozens of countries across the world. The game itself is as much a test of cunning as it is of knowledge. In the early rounds contestants answer questions to accumulate collective prize money; however, at the end of each round, one contestant is voted off, eventually leaving two contestants to compete for the cash. In order to win, it seems that players need to develop a clear strategy, hold their nerve, and of course possess good levels of knowledge—skills that anyone in the business of influencing others recognizes as important.

But is there another important but less obvious factor that could also influence who goes on to win the game?

When analyzing past episodes of the *Weakest Link*, social scientists Priya Raghubir and Ann Valenzuela found that contestants who stood in the two central positions in the show's familiar semi-circular shape were much more likely to win the game than contestants in the remaining positions. In other words, it wasn't just strategy, knowledge, and nerves of steel that played a part in winning the show—where a contestant stood also mattered.

The researchers found that this subtle yet important shift in location doesn't just serve to influence the outcome of TV game shows. They also found evidence that anyone who arranges to be located closer to a central position—for example, a recruiter in an interview panel, or executives in a meeting—gains influence over peers. Why? Raghubir and Valenzuela argue that one important reason is observers' learned associations and beliefs that the most important people are *expected* to be located in the center. Think of the bride and bridegroom at a wedding party, a CEO at a board meeting, and the gold medal–winning athlete at the Olympics.

Not only do we expect the important people to be located "in the middle," there is also worrisome evidence that, due to their central position, we are less likely to pay attention to the errors and mistakes they make. These findings have implications for meeting leaders who could find a hastily suggested proposal less challenged if it comes from someone who—by virtue of their seating position—is literally the "center of *in*attention."

Of course in those situations where it is your idea or proposition that you wish to promote, assuming that that idea or proposition is a good one, then a small change you could make to leverage-up your influence would simply be to seat yourself in a center position. And when speaking or presenting as a group, you could arrange for the centrally located person to deliver the statements you'd most like your audience to accept.

Not only does this research provide a useful reminder of why it is much better to consider the seating positions well before the start of a meeting, but additional research indicates that when it comes to presenting your products and services, such planning can make a real difference too. In one study designed to test this hypothesis, participants were asked to choose one of three differently flavored and simultaneously displayed packets of chewing gum. Even though the researchers routinely changed the order in which the packets were presented, it was the gum that was placed in the middle of the array that was selected most often, and by a significant margin. When the researchers extended the number of choices to five and also experimented not just with gum but with different varieties of other products too (that were all priced the same), they found the same result: *The option in the center stage position was selected significantly more often.*

Now while this finding might seem intuitive to some, we would wager that the demonstrated cause will be anything but intuitive. Contrary to what many people might think, the reason why the middle option is chosen more often has less to do with greater attention being drawn to options placed there or to the easier recall of products in those positions.

The primary reason that the center-positioned product was chosen most often was people's beliefs that products that are positioned in the center of an array are *deliberately* placed there because they are the most popular. Recall from previous chapters how, especially when someone is uncertain of what the best choice to make is, a choice becomes more compelling when it has been visibly popular with others. Note that in this study what signaled the product's popularity was not information about how popular it was at all, but rather its position in an array.

This explanation offers a way for manufacturers of truly popular products to ensure that they don't lose that earned influence via the politics of store shelf placements, which can sometimes be determined by payments to store managers. They can place the words "Best Selling" or "Most Popular" directly on their packaging, thereby communicating honestly which of the brands has "the strongest link" to genuine popularity, no matter where they are placed on the shelves.

CHAPTER 26

# What SMALL BIG can encourage more creative thinking?

A significant amount of research has demonstrated the remarkable influence that environments and surroundings can have on our behaviors and decisions. For example, people tend to eat less food from the buffet if they are given smaller plates, give greater tips to food servers if a credit card logo appears on the tray containing the check, and vote more conservatively if the voting booth is located in a church rather than a school.

In each of these examples, the decisions made, and the behaviors enacted, didn't occur as a result of a direct request or appeal. Instead they were influenced by a single feature of the environment that then *primed* an automatic and unconscious change in behavior.

Besides influencing voting choices via voting location or reducing calorie intake via plate size (politicians and nutritionists take note), do other opportunities exist where a small change in the environment could lead to big differences? For example, how about in your next business meeting or negotiation?

Many organizations will host meetings to share best practices, generate new ideas between colleagues, and encourage new ways of thinking. If you have ever been to such a gathering you will likely recognize that a variety of environmental factors

131

can influence its success, from the number of people attending (including the personality traits of those individuals) down to the quality of the lunch buffet and the drinks being offered. But is there something else that could also influence a team's ability to think in a blue-sky way?

Researchers Joan Meyers-Levy and Juliet Zhu believed that ceiling height can have a *priming* effect, influencing people to think more conceptually and creatively when the ceiling is high but in a much more specific and constrained way when the ceiling is low.

In order to test their ideas, the researchers set up a series of studies in which participants were asked to solve a series of word jumbles (anagrams). One group solved the puzzles they were given in a room with a low ceiling height (8 feet), with the other group working in a room with a higher ceiling (10 feet). Some of the anagrams participants were asked to solve related to the concept of freedom and creativity—for example, words like *liberated, unlimited,* and *emancipated* were included. However, for others, the words related to the concept of confinement— for example, *restricted, bound,* and *restrained.*

The researchers found that the participants solved freedom-based anagrams quicker and the confinement-based anagrams slower when they were in the high-ceiling room. The opposite was the case in the room with the low ceiling; there, participants' response times when solving the confinement-based anagrams were quicker than the freedom-based ones. A follow-up study also found that the participants located in the high-ceiling room were able to make relational connections between abstract ideas—a key feature of creative thinking—much more easily than those in the low-ceiling room.

The results of this study suggest that when arranging your business meetings, team workshops, or training programs and a central goal of those meetings requires an element of creative thinking, then a small change you could make in advance would simply be to select a facility with high ceilings. Doing so could increase the chances that your group is *primed* to think in a less constrained way.

However, if the meeting you have called concerns working on a specific item or challenge where it is not new ideas you are looking to foster, but rather specific actions and plans, then selecting a room with a lower ceiling would be the way to go. If your meeting requires the group to first think creatively about new ideas and then specifically about how those tasks will be carried out, then selecting two rooms, while a little more expensive, might provide a worthwhile return on investment if it helps turn all the creative thinking into concrete plans and action.

But what if your next business meeting is a negotiation, which, in contrast to a meeting that seeks to generate ideas, is more concerned with generating profits? Might the environment where your negotiation is actually conducted influence certain behaviors that change the outcome of the deal? For example, are you likely to be more persuasive in a business negotiation that is done in your own office rather than in a venue less familiar to you?

In the next chapter we'll take a closer look at the potential answers persuasion science can provide to these questions.

CHAPTER 27

# How can a SMALL change in venue lead to BIG differences in your negotiations?

In 1989, at the end of the Cold War, two ships off the coast of Malta—the Soviet cruise ship *Maxim Gorky* and the United States navy cruiser *Belknap*—were the location for the Malta Summit between US president George H. W. Bush and USSR chairman Mikhail Gorbachev. In 1995, the Dayton Accords were signed after Bosnia and Herzegovina outlined a peace treaty held at the Wright-Patterson Air Force Base near Dayton, Ohio. The practice of seeking "neutral" territory when negotiating has a long history, dating back hundreds of years— for example, the Treaty of Tilsit between Napoleon I of France and Czar Alexander I of Russia was signed on a raft in the middle of the Neman River.

The practice of negotiating at neutral venues isn't just limited to international peace negotiations either. When conducting contract negotiations, union representatives will frequently seek out impartial premises, preferring hotel conference rooms to company headquarters.

In the last chapter we discussed how a small change in ceiling height can influence the creative outputs of a meeting. But now imagine that the purpose of your next business meeting is to generate *commercial* results rather than *creative* ones. Could a small change in the venue, so that negotiations are conducted in your own office rather than a less familiar venue, make a big difference too?

Put simply, is there a "home field advantage"?

Ask that question to a sports supporter and you'll get a clear answer: "Of course it matters." When a team plays at home there is a general expectation from their supporters that they should perform better than when they play that same opponent on the road. In fact, there is no need to take the fans' word for this; there is clear evidence to back this up. In practically every sport, other things being equal, teams with the "home field advantage" win more often.

Behavioral scientists Graham Brown and Markus Baer set out to answer whether what most sports fans intuitively know plays out in business too. They started out by recruiting pairs of individuals to take part in a series of contract negotiations, with one assigned the role of purchaser and the other the role of supplier. To replicate what happens in real life, a large part of the negotiation discussion centered on the price, with purchasers wanting to pay as little as possible and with suppliers wanting to charge as much as possible.

The researchers used a clever methodology to manipulate who had "home status" and who had "visitor status"—in other words, whether the negotiators were in their home territory or were visitors in their opponent's territory. Each of those awarded home status was given the chance to personalize the negotiation environment by displaying their name outside the office, choosing which chair they sat in, placing posters and postcards on the walls, putting details of upcoming activities on a whiteboard, and being the guardian of the office key.

While those with "home status" were preparing their offices, those with "visitor status" were placed in a temporary location and told that negotiations would take place in their opponent's office, which their opponent supposedly had for a completely unrelated task. Once the residents were ready, the "visitors" were brought in for the actual negotiation.

Consistent with evidence supporting the sports team home advantage, the researchers found that those negotiating in their home territory outperformed the visitors regardless of whether they were purchasers or sellers in the negotiation. This suggests that when it comes to being a persuasive negotiator, a seemingly small decision like where to hold the negotiation could have a much bigger impact on the outcome than you might at first think.

So what exactly is going on? In a sports stadium, 50,000 supporters can help sway a team's performance, not to mention exert influence over a referee's decisions, but neither of these factors could have played a role in these negotiations. Instead, and consistent with the ceiling-height studies described in the previous chapter, it was *the setting of the negotiation* that was having an effect. Relative to a neutral location, negotiating "at home" increases one's confidence in the negotiation, whereas negotiating "away" decreases it.

So next time you are invited to negotiate at an opponent's location, it may make sense to suggest a small change by agreeing to meet in a neutral location. Better still, ask them to come to *your* office, recognizing that not only will the chances of scoring a better outcome be enhanced, but so will the chances that your colleagues, like any home crowd, will go wild when they hear of your success.

## CHAPTER 28

# What SMALL BIG can improve both your power and your persuasiveness?

In previous chapters we have explored the idea that certain features of an environment or surrounding can have a profound effect on behavior. People are more creative when the room they are in has a high ceiling compared to a low one because the environment subtly primes them to think in less constrained ways. College students give higher evaluation scores to their university lecturer if they have previously been given a hot rather than a cold drink, effectively priming them to literally feel warmer toward their tutor. And negotiators typically get more favorable outcomes if they arrange for deals to be struck on home soil.

In all these examples the small changes made to the environment or context had been arranged by a third party who recognized the big effect they could have without having to make people consciously aware of what was going on. But what if your goal is to influence your own behaviors rather than others'? For example, what small changes could jobseekers make in the way they prepare for a job interview that could spur them to perform better and increase their chances of getting their dream job?

Behavioral scientists Joris Lammers, David Dubois, Derek Rucker, and Adam Galinsky thought that one small change job applicants could make would be simply to think about a time when they felt powerful. The researchers set up a series of studies to test their ideas.

In one experiment, participants were assigned to the role of either a job applicant or interviewer. Before the interviews commenced, those assigned to the applicant roles were further divided into two groups and invited to carry out a warm-up task that they were told "would help them become familiar with writing about themselves." Half the applicants were given the task of writing about an experience in which they had felt powerful, but the other half were asked to write about an experience in which they had felt powerless.

Having been suitably encouraged to feel either powerful or powerless, the applicants were then shown a job advertisement for a sales analyst role that had recently appeared in a national newspaper. The researchers asked each applicant to assume that they possessed the relevant education and experience demanded for the role and to then write an application letter for this position. Having written the application letter, they were instructed to put it in a sealed envelope and to hand it to a research assistant.

Those application letters were then randomly distributed to the interviewers who, it is important to note, weren't aware of the writing task the applicants had been asked to undertake. The interviewers were instructed to read the applications carefully, forming an impression of the applicant and indicating how likely they would be to offer the candidate a job.

When the results were analyzed, it was clear that those applicants in the powerful group were much more likely to be offered a job by the interviewers than those in the powerless group, neatly demonstrating how the small act of writing about feeling powerful can make a big difference in the outcome.

But an argument could be made that this experiment only

measured the impact of this small change in a written application. It is perhaps unlikely that people in the job market
would be offered a position merely on the basis of a letter,
however well it might be written. The researchers had thought
of this, too. Recognizing that a face-to-face interview is often
the context in which decisions about job applicants are ultimately made, they set up another experiment where participants underwent a 15-minute interview to secure a place in a
business school.

The set-up for this second study was exactly as the first but
with one extra feature. In addition to the two groups who were
asked to write about a time when they either felt powerful or
powerless, the researchers added a third group as a control
condition that didn't carry out the writing task at all.

Following the interviews, the recruiters assessed the applicants' persuasiveness and then indicated whether they would
admit the applicant or not. Consistent with results from the
first experiment, writing about a time when they had previously
felt powerful had a big impact on how persuasive the applicant
was rated by the interviewer. Compared to the applicants in
the control condition, high-power applicants were seen as more
persuasive and low-power applicants as less persuasive. It was
these differences in persuasiveness that ultimately influenced
the overall outcome, and did so by a big margin.

Just under half of those in the control condition who were
interviewed were accepted. Only 26 percent of applicants who
were asked to write about a time when they felt powerless were
accepted. Now compare that figure to the close to 70 percent of
applicants who wrote about the time when they felt powerful
that were accepted.

Put a different way, recollected power increased the odds of
acceptance by 81 percent compared to the control group and by
a massive 162 percent compared to the low-power group.

Beyond an obvious small change that you can make when it comes to interviewing for that new promotion or pitching to a new client, these studies have potentially significant implications for recruitment agencies and job centers, too, who could help jobseekers have better interviews by encouraging them to consider and then write down times when they felt powerful. This might be especially important for those who have been unemployed for an extended period. Note, too, that in addition to having people write these things down, it will be important to time this exercise optimally, which, in the case of a job interview, should be shortly before it takes place and not hours, or even days, before.

Interestingly, research conducted by psychologists Dana Carney, Amy Cuddy, and Andy Yap suggests another potent way to make people feel more powerful: Have them adopt a high-power physical posture. Carney and her colleagues noted that two nonverbal body language dimensions are typically linked to high or low power: expansiveness (the amount of space that one's body takes up) and openness (whether the limbs tend to be open or closed). Whereas high-power individuals tend to assume expansive and open postures, low-power individuals tend to assume postures that are more constricted and closed.

In their study, the researchers told participants who came to the laboratory that the study was designed to test how the placement of electrodes at different places on the body could influence physiological recordings. In truth, Carney and her colleagues used this cover story as the rationale to ask the participants to pose in one of several different manners. The researchers found that participants who were asked to pose in an expansive and open way (for example, by leaning over a desk with their hands firmly planted on it, or sitting in a chair with their arms behind their heads and their feet on the desk) felt more powerful than those who were asked to pose in a more constricted and closed way (such as by sitting in a chair and crossing their arms and ankles).

Even more fascinating, those asked to engage in the high-power poses were found to have elevated testosterone (a hormone related to dominance) and reduced cortisol (a hormone related to stress). This research shows how such a minor change—how you position your body—can make a significant difference, not only psychologically but also physiologically.

Does this mean that Carney, Cuddy, and Yap would recommend that when you are being interviewed you put your shoes up on your interviewer's desk? Of course not. But their research suggests that if you do it during a phone interview or shortly before your in-person interview, you're likely to feel more confident, and that confidence might just be the seemingly small difference that helps you land that big job.

## CHAPTER 29

# Why might love be the only SMALL BIG you need?

On 25 June 1967, an estimated 400 million people from around the globe tuned in to the world's first-ever live satellite television broadcast, *Our World*. For two and a half hours, it showcased artists from close to twenty countries in an eclectic mix of performances, from opera singers and choir boys to ranchers herding cattle, interspersed with occasional educational segments explaining the workings of the Tokyo subway system and the world clock. It was the closing of this broadcast, however, that was etched into the memories of most viewers.

Having been tasked by the British Broadcasting Corporation to perform a song with an underlying message that would be understood by all, The Beatles performed "All You Need Is Love." Given that the broadcast occurred at the height of the Vietnam War, some speculated that the song was a not-so-subtle attempt by the song's author, John Lennon, to deliver propaganda through his art. Regardless, whatever underlying motivations may or may not have existed, few argued with Lennon's assertion to both the connecting and healing qualities of love.

As a team of persuasion scientists and practitioners, we would assert that love has influencing qualities too. Thankfully, you'll be relieved to learn that we are not about to suggest that you need to sing to the whole world. Instead we are going to suggest you do something much, much smaller, and that is simply to accompany your influence attempt with a single cue that acts as a signal for love.

Since the dawn of time there can be no doubting the extraordinary influence that the concept of love has had and continues to have on our lives. It is perhaps surprising then that at least until recently relatively few studies have tried to demonstrate the effects of love thoughts on persuasion.

In one study, conducted by the French behavioral psychologists Jacques Fischer-Lokou, Lubomir Lamy, and Nicolas Guéguen, pedestrians walking alone were stopped on a shopping street to participate in a survey in which they were asked to remember either a meaningful episode of love or a meaningful piece of music in their lives. After they had completed the survey and had walked on for a few minutes, the pedestrians were approached by a person holding a map and asking for directions. Those individuals who had previously been cued to think about the concept of love were significantly more helpful in the amount of time they were willing to spend in the effort.

In another set of studies, Guéguen and Lamy have shown how the simple action of including the word *love* on charitable appeals can lead to significant increases in donations. When researchers added the words donating = helping to standard charity collection boxes, they measured a 14 percent increase in donations compared to collection boxes that simply had information about the appeal. However, when the word *helping* was changed to *loving*, so the sign read donating = loving, donations increased by over 90 percent. That's a pretty impressive uplift for a small BIG that required a change to just one single word.

Food servers can benefit from the persuasive merits of love, too. In one experiment conducted by Guéguen, when the time came to settle the check, the food server placed the bill, which had been folded in half and placed under a plate, on the table. They then put two candies on top of the plate and left the area. Guéguen's team carried out this exercise hundreds of times, and at the end of the study period analyzed the data to see what influence this change had on diners' tips. It was clear that one particular group of diners was not only much more likely to leave a tip, but to leave a significantly larger tip, too. So what was persuading them to do this?

You could be forgiven for thinking that it had something to do with the two candies placed on the plate. Perhaps they were wrapped in red foil, a color synonymous with its connection to love, or maybe the candy was shaped like a heart. But the diners' increased tipping behavior had nothing to do with the candies at all, and instead had everything to do with the shape of the plate that their check was placed under. Unbeknownst to them, there were three different-shaped plates—round, square, and cardioid (heart-shaped). Those diners whose bills arrived on the heart-shaped plate left tips that were 17 percent higher than those whose checks came on a round plate, and 15 percent higher than the diners who got their checks on the square plate.

So what is going on? The researchers believe that when people are exposed to a sign that is synonymous with love— which, in the case of the restaurant, was a heart-shaped plate— it serves as a cue that activates other behaviors associated with love. And in this case, those were the helping and giving behaviors connected to tipping.

If this love association can increase the tips of a waiter or waitress who delivers the bill on a heart-shaped plate (or maybe even just draws a heart on the check itself), perhaps charity shops could increase the sale of secondhand clothing in their stores by simply changing the shape of the price tags from round or rectangular ones to heart-shaped ones. Fundraisers might include cardioid-shaped images on the donation pages of their websites. Your children might even increase the amount of money they raise for next week's swimming gala by prominently drawing a big red heart on the top of their sponsorship sheet before asking for sponsors.

# CHAPTER 30

# What SMALL BIG can help you find that perfect gift?

I f we were to ask a whole bunch of people how good they are at picking the perfect gift for a friend's birthday or a colleague's retirement, chances are that most of them would say they're quite good at it. Yet, if you asked those same people to rate the gift-giving skills of *their* friends, family, and coworkers, you would probably hear horror stories about them receiving all kinds of unintentionally hilarious items, from dubious hand-knitted sweaters to kitschy trinkets or electronic singing fish. In fact, if people were anywhere near as good at buying gifts for others as they think they are, then websites such as www. whydidyoubuymethat.com and www.badgiftemporium.com would be out of business.

Fortunately, researchers have discovered a remarkably simple strategy to ensure that yours is the gift that garners shrieks of delight and not gasps of horror.

According to a 2008 survey by the National Retail Federation almost 50 percent of Americans anticipate returning at least one holiday gift every year, a clear indication that gifts tend *not* to be nearly as cherished by recipients as gift givers might think. Noting this rather staggering statistic, researchers Francesca Gino (author of the excellent book *Sidetracked*) and Frank Flynn were interested in exploring the question of why gift givers and gift receivers so rarely see eye-to-eye on the quality or usefulness of a gift. They also thought that there was a simple solution to solving this problem: Prospective gift givers should just ask their friends, family, and coworkers to list some things they might like to receive and then buy something on the list for them.

One concern with having to ask the recipient what he or she wants is that it might signal that the giver doesn't know the recipient well enough to buy a personalized gift. Or perhaps worse still, that the gift giver doesn't really want to spend the personal time, effort, or energy necessary to choose a suitable gift. However, Gino and Flynn suspected that those who received the gifts would actually perceive the gift giver as *more* thoughtful for buying them something they really wanted.

In one study, Gino and Flynn took a group of married individuals and asked half of them to think about a time when they gave a wedding gift to someone else. The rest of the married people were asked to think about the wedding gifts they themselves had received. In addition, half of the people thinking about giving gifts were asked to think of a gift they chose from the registry, whereas the other half of the givers were asked to think of a gift they bought that was *not* on the registry.

Similarly, half of the gift recipients were asked to think about a gift they received that was from their registry, whereas others were asked to think about one they received that was *not* from their registry.

Although the gifts people chose to think about were of roughly the same monetary value (they averaged out at approximately $120), their perceptions of the gifts differed in some pretty important ways. Specifically, it didn't matter to gift givers whether the gift they were thinking about was from the registry or not—they all assumed that recipients appreciated and liked the gifts roughly to the same degree. However, for those who were asked to consider a wedding gift they had received, the ones thinking about a gift from the registry were far more appreciative of that present than those who thought about a gift they had received that wasn't from the registry.

Although the common saying is "It's the thought that counts," this research shows that it's the thoughtless gifts—the ones that involve simply picking from the recipient's predetermined list—that count most of all. In a way this doesn't sound that surprising. Couples who are planning to get married are perhaps more appreciative when someone buys them something from a prescribed list because that list likely contains items they truly need for a new home—items that they wouldn't wish to miss out on or duplicate. No couple needs three cheese boards—unless of course they live in the state of Wisconsin or their names happen to be Mickey and Minnie.

But what happens when the gift-giving context is different—for example, if the gift is for a birthday rather than a wedding? The researchers thought of that, too, and conducted a number of additional studies that all showed the exact same pattern: Gift givers didn't think that a recipient's level of happiness and appreciation for a gift would be influenced by whether the recipient asked for the gift or not. But in fact recipients were clearly much happier and more appreciative when they received something that they had previously said they would like.

In another of their studies, Gino and Flynn randomly assigned participants to be gift givers or gift recipients. Each gift giver was anonymously paired with a gift recipient. Each recipient was asked to select ten $20 to $30 gifts from Amazon.com, which would be sent in list form to a gift giver. Half of the gift givers were told to pick something from the list that would be sent to the recipients, whereas the other half of the givers were told to buy something that was not on the list. Once again the researchers found that those who were told to buy something not on the list were as confident that the recipient would like the gift as those who were told to buy something on the list. Yet, when the researchers looked at the recipients' evaluations, recipients who got something from their list were much more appreciative of the item.

Because the level of appreciation for a gift is one of the main determinants of not just how much receivers are motivated to reciprocate in the future but also how happy they are, this research has important implications for our interactions with others. As these findings show, making a small change that helps to take the guesswork out of gift giving by finding ways to identify the gifts people will truly appreciate is a win-win proposition for everyone involved. Providing a supply of sticky notes for a gift recipient to highlight desirable future presents they have spotted in magazines might be one strategy. Another would be to look out for the tell-tale signs of dog-eared pages in catalogues lying around the house.

The same should be true in a business context—for example, taking a client to that new lunch place they have mentioned a couple of times rather than the place you like best. Regardless, taking steps to buy from *their* list rather than yours is a small change that could lead to a big difference in appreciation. It will also go some way to ensuring that your dubious gift doesn't end up on the web, in the garbage can, or, perhaps worst of all, in your gift pile next year.

## CHAPTER 31

# What BIG advantages can you gain when you take the SMALL step of arranging to exchange?

Research has long demonstrated the value of a generous spirit. After providing gifts, favors, services, or assistance to others, we become more liked, more appreciated, and even physically healthier. What's more, those who have received from us typically stand ready to repay when we need something from them. This last benefit flows from the rule for *reciprocation*, which prescribes the willingness of people to pay back the form of behavior they have first received.

All human societies instill this rule in their members from childhood for a simple reason: It confers great competitive advantages on a group by encouraging profitable exchanges and mutually beneficial trade-offs between group members in vital arenas of interaction such as commerce, defense, and care. In the context of a workplace environment, this means that if you've complied with a colleague's request for help on one of their projects—let's say by providing effort, resources, or special information—then they should be significantly more willing to comply with a request for help that you might make of them in the future on a project that's important to you.

With so many of the reasons for being a giver securely in the plus column, it would be easy to think that a large amount of giving on the job is the surefire route to success. Unfortunately, human psychology is almost never so simple. The truth is, too much of a good thing can be a bad thing, even in the case of assistance. Take as evidence a study done by organizational psychologist Frank Flynn, who examined the consequences of favor-doing among employees at a large telecommunications firm. He measured the number of favors that workers did for one another along with a pair of noteworthy consequences. The first was the effect of favor-doing on the giver's social status within the organization—in other words, the giver's perceived worth to the company in the eyes of his or her coworkers. As you might have expected, those employees who were rated as more generous with their time, energy, and assistance to others were seen as more valuable. Achieving acknowledged social status in the workplace is no small feat and is a testament to the interpersonal gains that come from being a prodigious giver.

But the second consequence of giving that Flynn examined—productivity on the job—did not paint so sunny a picture. Eight measures of individual productivity, including assessments of both the quantity and quality of assigned work, showed that those employees with the highest-rated levels of assistance were significantly *less productive* than their colleagues. Why? Because they were so busy lending aid to others' projects that they were unable to pay sufficient attention to their own.

What are we to make of this state of affairs? If being a particularly openhanded giver on the job results in high social status but simultaneously reduces one's personal productivity on assigned tasks, what are we best advised to do? It turns out that there is a clear answer, one that emerged from another component of Flynn's study. It identified a small single factor that amplified both the social status and the productivity of a giver. That single factor wasn't the number of favors done. Instead, it was the *number of favors exchanged*. Employees who first provided beneficial aid on coworkers' projects and then got beneficial aid in return maximized the profitable effects of the giving process—not just for themselves but for everyone concerned—by rating high on both status and production. Recall, this outcome is very much in keeping with the rule for reciprocity that is vital to all successful groups precisely because it fosters mutually advantageous exchanges.

The implications of these results for each of us are clear. First, we should be liberal and proactive givers on the job. And note the crucial importance of being the first movers in the process. Going first activates the rule for reciprocity and thereby boosts the potential number of favor exchanges that are so central to mutual success in the workplace.

Second, it is important to characterize the help provided, assistance given, or valuable information delivered in ways that heighten the likelihood that it will be reciprocated fully in the future. This requires making a small, but important, change to the all-too-common response that we typically give when people thank us for our efforts. It is a change that has the ability to provide some startlingly big improvements both in terms of future cooperation and future influence attempts. Here are three suggestions for possible changes to your response, each to be offered upon receiving thanks for help you have given first.

1. "I was happy to help because I know how valuable it would be to get help if I were to ever need it."
2. "You're welcome. It's what colleagues do for one another."
3. "Of course. I know that if the situation were ever reversed, you'd do the same for me."

In summary then, the key to optimizing the giving process in the workplace is *to arrange for exchange*, which itself involves two small but crucial steps that can make for big differences: (a) Be the first to give favors, offer information, or provide service, and (b) be sure to verbally position your favor, information, or service as part of a natural and equitable reciprocal arrangement.

There is another important implication of this research as well. As Flynn points out, as part of their formal performance evaluation process, many organizations ask managers to rate their employees on numerous factors, including how much help employees provide to their colleagues. Flynn suggests that managers should formally evaluate employees not just on how much help they give to others, but also on how often they ask for help from others. Communicating both criteria to the organization's workforce, along with an explanation about why both are important, should go a long way to maximizing productivity by encouraging the provision of help as well as requests for help throughout the organization.

As authors, we hope that you will find a lot of benefit applying these small BIGs both in your professional as well as your personal lives, and if you found this chapter to be particularly helpful, please let us respond by saying, "[choose here from 1–3 above]."

## CHAPTER 32

# How could the SMALL act of showing your appreciation make a BIG difference when influencing others?

In the previous chapter we discussed how proactively seeking to help others and then characterizing that help in a way that heightens the likelihood of future exchanges can be a highly effective way to increase your influence—not just in that moment of obligation, but in the future, too. Because the principle of reciprocation encourages people to give back after they have received, the act of giving first is an especially good tool when seeking to develop new relationships, create engagement across teams, and develop long-term partnerships and opportunities with others.

But the rule for reciprocation is not a one-way street. While there are considerable advantages for influence afforded to favor-givers, what sometimes gets overlooked is the considerable opportunity for influence that exists for favor recipients.

Behavioral scientists Adam Grant and Francesca Gino thought that one way that the receiver of a good deed could increase his or her influence would be to explicitly convey gratitude toward the person or group who performed that initial favor. In one experiment in which the scientists tested this idea, participants were contacted via email and asked to spend time reviewing and then giving feedback to someone about a cover letter they had written for a job application. After sending in their feedback and comments, the participants received a second request from the cover letter author to read another cover letter.

However, this email took one of two different forms. In the control condition, the person who received the feedback simply sent back a note of acknowledgment as well as the new request. In the gratitude condition, however, the cover letter author sent back the exact same email, except in this one expressed a great deal of appreciation. ("Thank you so much! I am really grateful.")

So what was the effect of the small addition of these eight words? The researchers found that this explicit display of appreciation *more than doubled* the compliance rates for the new request.

But Grant and Gino weren't done yet. They also were interested in seeing whether expressing gratitude to a favor-doer had more wide-reaching effects. In particular, the researchers asked whether expressing gratitude toward a favor-doer could increase the favor-doer's motivation to help others in general. To do this, they ran a second experiment that was similar to the first in many aspects: The participants helped one particular student by giving him feedback on a cover letter, and that student either simply acknowledged the feedback or clearly conveyed gratitude for the feedback. However, in this experiment, instead of the original favor recipient asking for another favor, a complete stranger asked for the (second) favor.

Again, the researchers found that the compliance rate more than doubled in the gratitude condition.

Consider the significance of this finding. Simply expressing sincere gratitude toward a favor-doer actually doubled the chances that the favor-doer would subsequently help out a complete stranger. Additional data that Grant and Gino gathered suggests strongly that this occurs because expressing gratitude increases the favor-doer's overall sense of social worth—in other words, after receiving a signal of appreciation, favor-doers are more likely to feel that others value them.

But it is worth asking whether these impressive findings could be replicated outside of the laboratory in a fast-paced, real-life working environment. Grant and Gino thought that they could, so they set about testing these same ideas to measure how a genuine expression of gratitude might positively influence employee motivation. They chose to do so at a fundraising call center because they knew that fundraising can be a particularly thankless job, often characterized by frequent negativity and rejection.

In the experiment, half of the employees went about their day normally without any novel intervention; this was the control condition. However, for the other half, the director of annual giving visited the call center and thanked the fundraisers for the work they were doing. Specifically, she said, "I am very grateful for your hard work. We sincerely appreciate your contributions to the university." That's it. No handshakes, no hugs, no thank-you gifts—just sixteen straightforward words.

The researchers were able to monitor the number of calls the fundraisers made before and after this intervention took place. Whereas the employees in the control condition continued to make phone calls at the same rate, those in the gratitude condition made 50 percent more phone calls in the week following the director's visit. Imagine the impact of this small but important change. Even if the extra calls made remained largely similar in terms of their effectiveness, the fact that their number substantially increased likely swelled donations.

This research highlights how much positive impact can come from the seemingly small act of communicating your appreciation for the favors done and the efforts made on your behalf. Although it might seem obvious, think how often you may have responded with a mechanical "thanks" without truly showing how really grateful you are or without providing any additional information for why exactly you've been appreciative for help. Or how many times you intended to send a thank-you note to someone but somehow never got around to it. Not only are these missed opportunities for communicating your genuine appreciation, they are also missed opportunities for future influence.

This research suggests that managers and organizations stand to benefit by actively seeking out opportunities to provide explicit thanks. Doing so could serve to engender a culture of appreciation across their workplaces, inspiring additional organizational good citizenship behaviors throughout their companies.

There is a potential for policy makers and civil servants to prosper from the small act of showing appreciation, too. Recognizing and thanking citizens for the role they play in keeping streets clean, neighborhoods safe, and recycling rates high could prove to be a lot cheaper than the costs associated with incentivizing those types of behaviors or the remedial work required when less appreciation is shown.

Whether that means you'll be receiving a "Thank you for paying your taxes" card from the Internal Revenue Service or your city council anytime soon remains to be seen.

We bet you'd appreciate it though.

## CHAPTER 33

# Could unexpectedness be the SMALL seed that reaps a BIG harvest?

For worshippers gathering for weekly prayers at St. John's Church in the parish of Kirkheaton, a Yorkshire village in Northern England, it seemed like any normal Sunday morning. Even the November weather was typical—the sky was clear but the temperature cold, signaling the onset of a rapidly approaching winter. Removing hats and coats as they entered the church, some regulars nodded in polite recognition to fellow churchgoers as they took their seats. For many it would be the same seat that they had occupied in previous weeks and months. Even years.

Nothing at all appeared to be out of the ordinary.

However, for the rector of the church, the Reverend Richard Steel, that Sunday morning in 2012 was going to be anything but ordinary. He had a challenge on his hands. For the past seven years he had been leading a campaign to raise money for repairs to his Victorian-era church. It was a campaign that had been pretty successful, generating almost £500,000 ($750,000) through a variety of donations, charity appeals, and fundraisers. But old churches are expensive to maintain and tend to soak up funds at a rate that even the most tenacious and persuasive of clergy will struggle to replenish. Reverend Steel knew that despite his best efforts, half a million pounds, although impressive, was sadly not enough. The time had come to lead another push to raise more money. But how? What could he do to persuade his congregation, a group that had already contributed so much over the years, to pull together again in a concerted effort to raise the funds required to complete the restoration?

The strategy he adopted was both inspirational and extraordinary. It was a strategy that not only provided his church with the cash it needed to continue its restoration efforts, but also provided a wonderful demonstration of how to successfully deploy a fundamental principle of influence.

Reverend Steel decided that he was going to *give away* the church's money.

Tradition holds that at some point during a church service, members of the congregation will be expected to delve into a pocket, purse, or wallet and place a contribution into the collection box or on the collection plate being passed around. But, as the reverend explained to his bemused audience, today's collection would be rather different. Instead of asking his congregation to make a contribution to the collection plate, he requested that they make a *withdrawal* from it. And at that point, to the astonishment of almost everyone, a collection plate full of crisp £10 bank notes (roughly $15) was passed around the church and all in attendance were invited to take one.

At the end of this extraordinary "uncollection," having given away £550 (about $825) of the church's money, the reverend told his congregation that they were free to invest the £10 in any way they saw fit in the pursuit of generating a return that he hoped they would choose to give back to the church at a future date.

It takes a brave rector to give away his establishment's resources. It also takes an insightful one to do so in the way Reverend Steel did.

The act of providing resources to others first activates a fundamental principle of the influence process—namely, reciprocation. As we have already discussed in previous chapters, the principle of reciprocity evokes a powerful sense of obligation that recipients feel to repay, in kind, what has been provided to them first—a sense often accompanied by a healthy return. Marketers know that the offer of a free sample can lead to a larger purchase that more than compensates for the cost of their initial "gift." Smart leaders recognize that, by being the first to listen, offer assistance, and proactively identify those that they can help rather than those that can help them, they can increase the success of future influence attempts. Consistent with the theme of this book, these initial actions can be small, often costless. However the return on these small investments can be disproportionately large, stimulating loyal customers and productive colleague relationships primarily due to the creation of a network of willing others.

It's not just savvy marketers and managers who understand the powerful sway of the reciprocity principle. Sociologists too have recognized that in every society there is an obligation to give, to receive, and to repay. It is an expectation founded in society's golden rule, which, as part of the socialization process, advises that we all "give unto others as you would have them give to you." Notice that the golden rule doesn't state "Give unto others as *they* have given to you." Tellingly, the rule advocates that the influencer always take the first step. It was this first step—the action of giving first rather than taking—that Reverend Steel ably demonstrated in his expertly executed influence strategy.

But there was something else, crucial to the success of his strategy, that Reverend Steel recognized.

Although it may be the case that society obliges all of us to give back to others in the form of behavior, gift, or service we have first been given, it is also true that modern life is so over-crowded with experiences that it can be difficult to distinguish among the many different resources we have been afforded in the first place. The ubiquity of free trials and samples will often crowd out other free trials and samples. Valuable information can quickly be overshadowed by other valuable, and competing, information. The provision of help and assistance to a customer or a coworker might quickly be trumped by help and assistance provided by a competitor or a colleague.

In such a context it is both saddening and sobering to recognize that, nowadays, simply being the first to give often just won't be enough. Increasingly an additional ingredient is needed in order to bolster efforts so that they rise above the efforts of others. What's remarkable about this key ingredient is how small and underutilized it can be, sometimes going completely unrecognized while generating large payoffs.

That key ingredient is *unexpectedness.*

The impact of giving a gift, service, or even information first and in an unexpected way can have a huge impact. In our earlier book, *Yes!*, we described one study that demonstrated how food servers in restaurants could modestly increase the level of gratuities they received (by 3.3 percent) by leaving a candy for each diner when they brought the bill. If they leave two candies, tips increase further (by 14.1 percent). But a third approach showed that doing something unexpected could lead to even more impressive results. After leaving a single candy for each diner at the table, if that same server returned with a second candy *a few moments later,* the unexpectedness of this extra gift led to an impressive 21 percent increase in tips.

It's not just food servers who stand to benefit from the powerful influence of an unexpected gift or favor. A study conducted by consumer researchers Carrie Heilman, Kent Nakamoto, and Ambar Rao found that supermarket customers spent an average of 11 percent more on their shopping when they were offered surprise coupons after entering the store compared to coupons provided beforehand. It would seem that retailers might stand to profit handsomely simply by changing the timing of when vouchers or coupons are distributed. The unexpected nature of this "gift" serves to amplify a customer's positive response.

It was recognizing this important shift, from giving first in an *expected* way to giving first in an *unexpected* way, that served Reverend Steel so well. Sure, he could have invited some of his congregation to a meeting to brainstorm new fundraising ideas, making sure to provide coffee and cookies first in an effort to oblige more people to attend. Such an approach could be considered an example of reciprocity in action yet would have been unlikely to match the kind of response that his strategy ultimately generated.

The lessons seem clear. Although being the first to give or offer help will likely carry some sway, the optimal use of this fundamental principle of influence lies in ensuring that what you give first is unexpected relative to the norm. Writing a handwritten note rather than a typed one. Sending a personalized "Looking forward to doing business with you" card to a new client. Proactively asking if you can help your colleague on an important work assignment.

These may seem like small changes, but they can very often lead to much-improved results.

Speaking of results, what came of Reverend Steel's initial £550 ($825) investment? Six months after that unexpected Sunday morning service, a local BBC news team that had covered the original story returned to Kirkheaton to find out. What they discovered was nothing short of astonishing. Pretty much everyone who accepted the £10 had put the money to good use, some in extremely enterprising ways. One group used the money to buy ingredients to bake cakes and then held a bake sale. One person used the money to advertise a dog-walking service, raising funds in the process. A group of children from the local school pooled their money to buy seeds and then sold the resulting produce at a nice markup. Others used the money to buy goods from eBay that they resold and then returned their profits to the church. In just six months Reverend Steel's initial investment in his congregation yielded £10,000 ($15,000)—an almost twenty-fold return!

That's a pretty impressive return on investment. And a wonderful example of a small BIG.

## CHAPTER 34

# What surprisingly simple SMALL BIG can get you the help you need?

The answer is…just ask! That may seem like an enormously obvious assertion, but consider some research conducted by the social scientists Frank Flynn and Vanessa Bohns. They suggested that people who are thinking of making a request have a tendency to underestimate the likelihood that the recipient of their request will actually say yes. They conducted a number of studies to test their idea.

In one study, participants were told that their task was to ask strangers if they would be willing to fill out a questionnaire. Before the participants went out to complete this task, they were asked to predict the likelihood that a given person would agree to the request. Specifically, they had to estimate how many people they likely would have to ask before five people agreed. Although, on average, participants estimated that it would take asking just over 20 strangers, in fact it took just over 10. In essence, the participants underestimated the likelihood of agreement by about half.

Flynn and Bohns found similar results with lots of other types of requests, including asking strangers to walk them to the local gym and to lend them their cell phones to make a quick call. In another especially interesting study, the researchers selected a group of participants who were going to raise funds

164

for charity. Before the fundraising began, Flynn and Bohns asked the participants to estimate the likelihood that the people they approached with a donation request would give. Once again, the fundraisers underestimated by nearly half. In fact, they also underestimated the average amount that each person would donate by about 25 percent.

The authors collected additional data to determine exactly why people have this strong tendency to underestimate the likelihood that a person will respond affirmatively to a request for assistance. In brief, they found that requesters tend to focus on the cost to the potential help-provider in terms of time, effort, or money if he or she says yes, while giving less consideration than they should to the "social costs" (in terms of the difficulty, awkwardness, or potential guilt/embarrassment) the potential help-provider will experience if he or she says no.

The implications seem clear. When trying to decide whether to make a request of someone, it's important to recognize that you might be underestimating the likelihood of hearing yes. This underestimation, if left uncorrected, could therefore potentially stymie your productivity or the accomplishment of your goals.

Moreover, for those in managerial and team leader roles, the results of these studies should be particularly startling because they suggest that there may be situations when members of your team need help on a critical project but they may incorrectly assume that you are unlikely to give that help if they ask. To reduce the likelihood that this will occur, you would be well advised to make certain that your subordinates, coworkers, and team members are aware of your willingness to give them assistance where needed. How? By describing the findings of Flynn and Bohns and telling team members that you want to ensure that this kind of misperception doesn't undermine anyone's performance in your group.

In another set of studies, Bohns and Flynn suggest an additional reason why needed help often doesn't occur. Not only is it the case that requesters tend to *underestimate* the likelihood that a request for help will result in a yes, those helpers who are standing ready to help tend to *overestimate* the likelihood that a person will ask for help if they need it, leading to a double whammy that only has downsides. Those who need help don't ask. Those who can help don't offer, because they wrongly assume their help isn't needed simply because it wasn't asked for.

As a result, a common trap that managers and team leaders must avoid when communicating their willingness to help is not just to emphasize the practical benefits afforded to those who ask for help. They should also take steps to assuage in advance the potential feelings of any discomfort or embarrassment that help-seekers might experience by having to ask. Astute managers will do this by pointing to a past situation when they were glad they asked for help, ensuring that they also report how asking wasn't anywhere as embarrassing as they thought it would be. Healthcare professionals, keen to encourage their patients to continue seeking help and information, should find that adding to their offer of help a small signal of reassurance—like "There are no silly questions"—could make a big difference.

You might even decide to send them a copy of this chapter, remembering how the small act of personalizing it by handwriting their name across the top could lead to an even BIGGER difference.

## CHAPTER 35

# What SMALL BIG can make the difference when it comes to effective negotiation?

Sometimes the first few minutes at the negotiating table can seem a little like the first few minutes in the boxing ring: both opponents dancing around, reluctant to put themselves out there and make the first move. Just as some boxers are reluctant to throw the first punch, negotiators are often reluctant to put the first offer on the table. From a certain viewpoint this is understandable. They may be worried that being the first to make an offer will telegraph their strategy, or that doing so will perhaps reveal some sort of vulnerability.

But are they right to think in this way? When it comes to negotiation, or pretty much any other situation where you wish to influence someone, is it better to make the first strategic move or should you instead let your opponent do so?

According to research conducted by social psychologists Adam Galinsky and Thomas Mussweiler, you're far better off making the first offer in a negotiation than letting your counterpart strike first.

In a series of experiments, the researchers found that regardless of whether the person's role in the negotiation was the buyer or the seller, negotiators who were given instructions to make the first offer typically obtained a superior outcome compared to those who were instructed to wait for their opponent to make the first offer. For example, in one of the experiments, when parties looking to buy a factory made the first offer, the sellers ultimately agreed to an average selling price of $19.7 million. On the other hand, when parties looking to sell the same factory made the first offer, the buyers ultimately agreed to an average price of $24.8 million. The researchers found similar results in the domain of salary negotiations as well.

So what is causing these big differences in negotiations to occur? The primary reason is that when negotiators present their first offer they also "anchor" the other party, perceptually, onto the initial numerical terms. As a result, even though the recipients should ideally determine the value of the negotiated items independent of the numbers provided by the initial offer, they very often don't. They instead use the opening number provided by their counterpart as an anchor, and then they subsequently insufficiently adjust away from those numbers as the negotiation continues.

Why does this happen? Consider the case of someone selling a used car to a potential buyer. When the seller first suggests a relatively high starting price, potential buyers automatically start to think about all of the information that's consistent with that high-priced anchor point. Recall how throughout the book we have discussed how individuals are motivated to make accurate decisions efficiently. With a very high initial price, the buyer might ask himself, "Why so high?" and wonder if he needs to correct a potentially inaccurate perception of the value of whatever is being negotiated.

In trying to answer that question, the buyer is likely to spontaneously focus on the features that are all in line with the initial high price—for example, the luxurious aspects of the car, its reliability, and great gas mileage. Now consider what would happen if the buyer had made the initial (and far lower) offer. The seller might answer his own "Why so low?" question by spontaneously focusing on features of the car that are consistent with the buyer's low anchor—for example, that the car has several noticeable dents and scratches, the overall mileage is high, and there's an "old car smell" that now makes him wish he had showered immediately after a hard workout at the gym instead of waiting until he drove home each morning to get clean.

Because it's the counterpart of the person who makes the initial offer who automatically starts thinking about the features of the initial offer, that person is likely to start thinking that the true value of whatever is being negotiated is actually closer to the initial offer than originally thought. Accordingly, regardless of whether your role is that of the buyer or the seller, or employer or employee negotiating over this year's raise, or manager or subordinate trying to come to an agreement on resource allocation, you should consider carefully what would constitute an appropriate anchor in your negotiations and then be the first to make that offer rather than wait for your negotiation partner to make theirs. As Galinsky and Mussweiler demonstrated in their studies, this small act of going first could lead to some big differences in the results you get.

While small, it's a change that could pay big dividends. Of course, you need to ensure that your initial offer is within the realm of reality, even if it is geared toward the limits of what is realistic. For example, it's probably unrealistic to set the initial price for your Honda Civic at $100,000, claiming that it has a one-of-a-kind scent that the buyer can't find elsewhere! But as long as your initial offer is within the bounds of reason, it's important to throw that first punch instead of allowing your opponent to do so. Failure to take advantage of such an opportunity may lead you to finding yourself down and out within a few minutes of the opening bell.

Parents take note. Be sure you get in the first bid with those bedtimes!

Of course, we recognize that you can't always beat your counterpart to the punch. Are there any strategies available in situations in which your opponent is the one who comes out swinging? For example, prospective home buyers have to deal with published list prices that are already established before anyone even begins to negotiate, and many companies tell individuals their starting salaries immediately after offering them their jobs. Fortunately, Galinsky and Mussweiler proposed and tested a rather simple but incredibly effective strategy for escaping this psychological trap: *Focus on your ideal price*, which will lead you to spontaneously consider information that's inconsistent with your opponent's anchor.

One easy way of doing this might be to come into the negotiation not only with your ideal price in mind, but also with a written list of why that ideal price is justifiable. Even if you don't bring up every one of these points in the negotiation explicitly, simply having it there in front of you may very well be a strong enough cue to counteract the otherwise automatic process of questioning whether one's own original judgment was accurate.

## CHAPTER 36

# Could precision be the SMALL BIG when it comes to better bargaining?

During the 2013 summer transfer period, English soccer club Arsenal FC offered to buy the Uruguayan striker Luis Suarez from their Premier League rivals Liverpool FC for the sum of £40,000,000 + £1. The precision of Arsenal's bid stuck out like the proverbial sore thumb (or should that be toe?) compared to the more typical round number transfer fees. It had been designed primarily to trigger a clause in Suarez's contract that entitled him to be informed of bids from other clubs that were in excess of £40 million. Despite their highly precise offer, Arsenal's bid failed.

In the previous chapter we talked about how the first offer made in a negotiation typically acts as an anchor serving to influence your opponent's subsequent offers and counteroffers. Should we therefore conclude that the reason Arsenal's bid failed (despite the fact that they made the first offer) was down to the preciseness of their opening bid? Certainly not. The Suarez situation was a lot more complex than a simple haggling over the numbers. But a claim could be made that because of the unusual preciseness of Arsenal's offer, it did serve another function—it piqued global interest and attention. Evidence to support this claim comes from the fact that the story itself ran for weeks and generated thousands of column inches in the sports pages (no doubt further fueled by the fact that Suarez already had a reputation for being a somewhat controversial player).

It turns out that there is another place we can turn, beyond the sports pages of the papers, for evidence not just of the attention-grabbing nature of a precise offer but also of the remarkable influence that precise opening offers can have in your negotiations. That place is, of course, persuasion science.

Behavioral scientist Malia Mason and her colleagues Alice Lee, Elizabeth Wiley, and Daniel Ames believed that people could improve the result of their negotiations not just by ensuring that they made the first offer, but also by ensuring that first offer was a precise one. In one study, participants were asked to read an account of a fictional negotiation concerning the sale of a used car. In each case the participants assumed the role of the seller and received one of three offers made to them by potential buyers. One offer was an even-number offer of $2,000 and the other two offers had precise endings: $1,865 and $2,135. After each participant received their opening offer, they were then asked to respond with a counteroffer of their own. Interestingly, those sellers given an initial offer that ended in a precise number were much more conciliatory with their counteroffer, typically countering with an offer 10 percent to 15 percent higher than the opening offer. However those given the $2,000 opening typically countered with an offer that represented a more than 23 percent difference. Given these results, it seems that the small extra act of providing a precise opening offer in a negotiation can be a potent strategy that potentially reduces the gap between the two parties as the negotiation progresses. Why?

The researchers thought that recipients of precise offers are much more likely to believe that the person making that offer has invested time and effort preparing for the negotiation and therefore has very good reasons to support the precise offer they are making. This was consistent with a subsequent test conducted by the researchers in which they measured participants' perceptions following the negotiations and found them likely to agree with statements such as "The young man put considerable energy into researching the value of the car" and "He must have had good reasons for the price he suggested."

It is also interesting to note that the researchers found that this effect was consistent regardless of whether the precise offer was higher or lower than the $2,000 round-ended opening offer. This insight leads to an intriguing thought that when the time comes to sell that uniquely scented Honda Civic that's taking up space on your driveway, you could end up financially better off by opening with a reduced but more precise offer of, say, $3,935 than a larger, less-precise one of $4,000. Of course should you be in the market for such a car you might be advised to pay special attention to the seller whose opening demand is unusually specific.

This precise number approach shouldn't just be reserved for one-off transactional negotiations such as selling that second-hand car. The researchers found similar results across a range of other negotiation contexts. For example, in a second experiment, experienced managers and executive MBAs were split into 130 pairs for a series of live negotiations. Consistent with the previous study, those executives who made an opening offer in the form of a precise number received counteroffers that were on average 24 percent closer to their opening offer than those who made a round-number offer. In every case this anchoring to the initial offer carried right through to the final settlement.

As we advocated in a previous chapter, one small change that a negotiator can make that can lead to improved results is to make the first offer. This research provides one extra small but important shift in approach that can lead to another big difference in outcome—making that first offer a precise one.

Accordingly, having already researched all the information, equipment, materials, and resources required to prepare that highly detailed proposal for a prospective client, don't make your subsequent negotiations harder by making the mistake of rounding up your quotation in the mistaken belief that doing so might make it easier for a prospective customer to process. Instead, present that precise number early on in your negotiations.

A similar approach should be taken when negotiating a review in your salary and benefits package. Although it may be easier and simpler to ask your boss for a raise of 10 percent, asking instead for a raise of 9.8 percent or 10.2 percent should result in less resistance due to the precision of the number. Of course, you should be prepared to justify why you are asking for that number—perhaps that is the exact average raise of everyone in your position at work. Similarly, a babysitter hoping to net an average hourly rate of $15 would be advised to open with an offer of $15.85 rather than $16 when negotiating with parents.

This kind of approach could also be useful when it comes to managing projects and persuading people to complete tasks by a certain time and date. This research would suggest that rather than asking people to get back to you in two weeks, you might get more timely responses if you actually stipulate 13 days. In a similar vein, rather than requesting that a job be completed by the close of the business day or by the end of the week, you might be more effective signaling a precise time: for example, "Could you please get this back to me by 3:47 p.m. on Thursday?" Not only might this small change result in more timely responses to your requests, it might also help you manage your email more effectively and get you back enough of your weekend that you can watch those overpaid professional athletes strut their stuff.

## CHAPTER 37

# Why might a SMALL change in number ending make a BIG difference to your communications?

A recent analysis of prices charged in a major American supermarket revealed an interesting fact. About 80 percent of the store's products were given a price ending in the number 9. This finding wasn't just limited to a single store or even a particular chain of stores. It seems that most retailers adopt a similar policy. The practice of pricing goods with odd-ended numbers is not a cultural anomaly solely reserved for the American market, either. Studies in Germany, Great Britain, and New Zealand have found similar pricing patterns.

So where did this strange practice of odd-ended pricing originate? One potential explanation can be traced back to the standardization of the American currency in 1891. When imported goods from Britain underwent a currency conversion from pounds to dollars, they would end up with an odd price. The perception that British goods were often considered to be of a higher quality meant that odd price endings became associated with a mark of superiority. Another commonly cited reason for the introduction of odd price endings was that it was a pretty good strategy to reduce employee theft. Odd pricing would force employees to issue change, therefore making it more difficult for them to pocket a payment without recording the transaction on a sales slip. Records show that when the department store Macy's adopted 99-cent sales in the early twentieth century, they reported a rise in sales, leading to the practice then being adopted by retailers around the world.

Given the almost ubiquitous practice of 99-cent prices it is interesting to note that another well-known retailer recently made the decision to buck this pricing norm. In 2011 Ron Johnson, a former senior vice president at Apple, joined JCPenney as its new CEO and a short time later launched an "Everyday" pricing policy across its stores. The cornerstone of his initiative was a decision to use whole numbers on price labels rather than the more familiar .99 endings. For example, a pair of denim shorts previously tagged at $18.99 or $19.99 would be priced at $19 or $20, respectively. The rationale given for the idea was a simple one: Prices ending in round numbers are clear and straightforward and convey a simple and honest message. JCPenney's small shift in pricing strategy, while a setback for the copper cent, would surely be a victory for common sense. Most importantly, though, JCPenney thought it would be a victory for their customers who would surely vote with their wallets.

And vote with their wallets they did. The following year JCPenney's sales tanked by almost 30 percent.

Given that the economy, at the time, was still in the early stages of recovery and could be described, at best, as fragile, it would be absurd to suggest that JCPenney's decision to move to round number price endings was wholly responsible for the monumental slump in its sales. There was likely a multitude of other factors that contributed to its nose-diving sales. But there is good evidence that JCPenney's "Everyday" pricing policy probably didn't help. And it certainly didn't help Mr. Johnson, who was soon removed from his CEO position.

At first glance the idea that shifting a customer's attention from a precise price ending (for example, $0.99) to a round price ending (for example, $1.00) appears to be one that should have little impact on whether a positive purchase decision is made or not. After all the difference is a paltry penny. The saying may advocate "take care of the pennies and the pounds will take care of themselves," but the value of a penny these days is so small it hardly seems worthy of attention at all.*

In such a context JCPenney's pricing shift should have made little if any difference. But as we have consistently shown in this book, small changes can lead to a big difference—even if that small change concerns one penny on a sales tag.

But why?

One reason is that a .99 price ending acts as a signal for "a good deal." Research by Charlotte Gaston-Breton and Lola Duque suggests that this can be especially effective with younger consumers or when there is low involvement in the decision to purchase, such as with lower-value items. Other research has found that products that have .99 endings tend to cause a "levelling down" effect when it comes to perceptions of price bands. In other words, a product sold at $19.99 can be categorized in the "less than $20" band but the moment it costs a penny more it's in the "$20 and above" band, creating a subtle but important contrast.

In addition to influencing the price category that a product falls into, a one-cent change in price ending might also serve to signal another important feature of the price—the left-most

---

*Given that the penny is typically the smallest denomination in most currencies, another common saying, "See a penny pick it up and all day long you'll have good luck," might prompt you to wonder whether picking up a penny off the street is worth the time and effort at all. It turns out economists have studied this and a clear answer emerges—it isn't. There's also no evidence to support the idea that finding a penny brings good luck either, but given that's a rather tricky thing to test, that's a decision you should probably take yourself leaving the scientists out of it.

number. In the previous example, not only does a product priced one cent cheaper at $19.99 fall into the "less than $20" category, but the left-most number also changes from 2 to 1. It turns out that this "left-digit effect" is important primarily because it is what people typically pay attention to first.

Researchers Kenneth Manning and David Sprott provide compelling evidence for how a small change in price ending that affects the left-most number in the price can have a dramatic influence on people's purchasing decisions. In Manning and Sprott's studies, participants were given the opportunity to purchase one of two pens that were presented to them side by side. Pen A was the lower-priced option and Pen B was the higher-priced option because of a couple of extra features it had. The participants were then asked to evaluate the two pens and make a choice about which one they would like to purchase. The researchers had assigned participants to one of four different price conditions:

|  | *Pen A* | *Pen B* |
|---|---|---|
| Condition 1 | $2.00 | $2.99 |
| Condition 2 | $2.00 | $3.00 |
| Condition 3 | $1.99 | $2.99 |
| Condition 4 | $1.99 | $3.00 |

Despite the fact that the difference across the first three price conditions was very small (there is just a one-cent difference between conditions 1 and 2) the impact was very large indeed. Pen A was selected by 56 percent of participants in condition 1, but by 69 percent in condition 2 and 70 percent in condition 3.

Why such a big uplift? Notice that compared to condition 1, where the left-most digit is the same for both Pen A ($2.00) and Pen B ($2.99), in conditions 2 and 3 the left-most digit is different, making Pen A seem like a much cheaper pen relative to Pen B in those two conditions.

But now let's consider condition 4, where a small change has resulted in the difference between the left-most digits being two dollars—Pen A ($1.99) and Pen B ($3.00). It turns out Pen A fared best of all with this combination, with nearly 82 percent of participants purchasing Pen A. This is a neat demonstration of how a small change to the left-most digit can have a big effect on resulting choices.

We bet that Ron Johnson now wishes he and the rest of the JCPenney team had understood the science of persuasion before embarking on his "Everyday" round-ended pricing policy. This research shows that changing the price of, say, a pair of socks from $8.99 to $9—that is, making it a penny more expensive—has the effect of making the socks actually seem nearly a dollar more expensive because consumers are so focused on the left-most digit.

More generally, the implications of this study have a variety of potential applications for those looking to influence the choices and decisions of others. Most obviously, those responsible for setting prices in retail environments may benefit from the knowledge that a small shift in price—which might literally be just one cent upwards or downwards—can disproportionately alter a consumer's judgment of the cost of that product as well as their purchasing decision. For example, a business that sells lower-priced, high-margin products such as own-brand goods may be able to improve their profitability by making small changes to the price endings of their products that increase the perceptual difference between the left-most digit of their price and that of a premium product. Of course, should it be the case that the goal is to increase the likelihood that people will choose a more expensive product, then the opposite would be true.

Notice that in the pen study many more folks chose the more expensive pen when the left-most digit was the same for both options.

Less obviously, there might be other ways to use the intriguing influence that numbers that are slightly less than whole numbers often have on others' decisions. A personal trainer might find that a client is a little more compliant to a training program framed as 9.9 kilometers on the treadmill rather than a round-ended 10 kilometers. A doctor may measure helpful differences in a patient's adherence to exercise by advocating a slightly lower number of steps on their pedometer— say 9,563 rather than the more usual 10,000. In these scenarios, these goals should seem disproportionately more attainable to the client or patient, and therefore they should be more motivated to work to achieve them.

Finally, a small change to the way times and agendas are framed may result in more acceptances and fewer declines for future meetings you are hosting. While speculative on our part, changing that upcoming 2-hour gathering to one that is scheduled for 1 hour 55 minutes might result in a few extra attendees.

Perhaps this small, but important, change informed by persuasion science will spawn a completely new approach when it comes to persuading people to attend your meetings. But before you think about contacting Apple, Microsoft, or Google to suggest they change the default settings on their electronic calendars, be aware that we have already copyrighted "The 29-Minute Meeting."

## CHAPTER 38

# Could a SMALL change in order be the BIG difference that wins you more orders?

In the mid-1970s Italian restaurateur and businessman Antonio Carluccio left his Northern Italian home and moved to the United Kingdom where, following stints as a wine importer and then working with Terence Conran's famous restaurant group, he opened his first food shop. Today there are more than 70 Carluccio cafes across Europe and the Middle East serving a range of authentic Italian foods including pastas, salads, gelatos, and...scooters!

Yes that's right. Prominently displayed on each Carluccio menu is a Vespa scooter that diners can order, presumably in a color of their choosing, while deciding what they might want to eat for dinner.

We are uncertain of exactly how many people would want to purchase a scooter from a restaurant. We are also unsure exactly how many Vespas have been sold in Carluccio's cafes. But there is one thing, as a team of persuasion scientists, which we are certain about—the potential influence that a big-priced item (a Vespa scooter costs around $3,500) might have on the much smaller priced food items found on the same menu. Carluccio may not be selling too many scooters in his cafes, but the small act of including it on his menus may mean he is selling a lot more top-end panini. Put simply, including the motorbike on his menu makes his sandwiches appear to be a better value.

People rarely make decisions in a vacuum; in other words, our choices are almost always influenced by context, whether that context involves the potential alternatives we're considering, aspects of the decision-making environment, or simply what we were thinking about before making the decision. As a result, the order in which options and choices are offered is really important. A basic concept in psychology is the phenomenon of *perceptual contrast*. This is the idea that a person's perception of an offer can be changed not by making changes to that offer at all, but instead by changing what the person experiences immediately before the offer is presented. A $35 bottle of wine seems expensive if it appears halfway down a list that begins with a house wine priced at, say, $15. However, that same $35 wine will appear much more reasonably priced if a small change is made to the list so that a more expensive wine, say one for $60, appears on the list first. Nothing changes about the wines—just the order in which they are presented.

Therefore one small change anyone can make to potentially increase the success of a presented proposal or an offer is to carefully consider what the target audience will be comparing the proposal or offer to when they are making the decision.

Interestingly, this strategy can be just as effective even when the comparisons are ones that your audience is going to reject anyway. For example, when constructing a proposal for a client, a management consultancy might weigh several alternative approaches and, through a process of elimination, converge on an optimal recommendation. At this point, having thrown the ideas they eliminated in the trash, many of which might be too costly or take too much time to complete for the client's liking, they would then work up the proposal focusing on their optimal choice. However, based on what we know about the persuasion process and specifically perceptual contrast, this would be a mistake.

Instead, the consultancy would be advised to take the ideas they decided to throw out and present them first, albeit briefly, at the start of their pitch. This small change could make for a big difference when it comes to presenting their chosen pitch because that proposal would now be seen in its proper perspective. For example, by first presenting an option that the client might think is a bit too costly, or one that the client might think will take too much time, will have the desired impact of making the target proposal seem even more like the "Goldilocks" proposal that it is—just right.

But what about situations when your offer or proposal is made up of multiple items bundled into packages? For example, a movie theatre might offer customers the option to watch 15 movies for $99. A lawyer might offer 10 hours of consulting time for $2,500. An online music retailer might charge $29.99 to download 70 songs. Will the purchase decisions be affected by which of the two numbers appears first? Put another way, and using the online music retailer as an example, would more people be tempted by an offer of 70 songs for $29.99 or an offer of $29.99 for 70 songs?

Researchers Rajesh Bagchi and Derick Davis conducted a series of experiments looking for answers to this very question. In one study participants were asked to consider one of a range of offers made by an on-demand TV broadcaster. One group received a price-then-item offer—specifically $300 for 600 hours of TV. A second group was offered an item-then-price offer—in this case 600 hours of TV for $300. Other groups, however, were presented with offers that comprised different combinations that were economically the same, including 60 hours for $30, $285.90 for 580 hours, and 580 hours for $285.90.

The resulting analysis showed that when an offer was easy to calculate, as was the case for the first and second experimental groups, it made little difference whether the item or the price came first. But when an offer was a little more difficult to calculate, things changed, with a preference for offers that were presented in the item-then-price sequence. This was especially the case if the package on offer was a large one. For example, people were more likely to prefer and trial the "580 hours for $285.90" offer than the "$285.90 for 580 hours" offer—despite these offers being exactly the same.

Why? It seems that as choices increase in complexity our attention is directed to the very first piece of information presented, be it the number of items, price, amount of time, or any other unit or measurement. In this case, people's evaluations of the deal were more positive because the benefits were listed first and the cost was listed second. Furthermore this effect is amplified as it becomes more difficult to calculate what is being offered, ultimately leading to different evaluations and preferences for things that are the same.

There is a practical and potentially useful lesson for anyone in business to consider. Imagine, for example, that you are putting together a proposal for a client to supply a range of consultancy services over a period of time. Your proposal is quite complex involving multiple people delivering a variety of services at different rates, at different times, and in separate locations. In such situations this study, and others like it, suggest a small yet important shift in your approach to ensure you lead with an item-then-price strategy.

But what about situations where the offer you are making is much easier to calculate or involves smaller numbers of units? Even though these studies suggest that these order effects might be less pronounced, the process of attending to what you offer first remains highly relevant. And given the potentially big uplifts that can result in your subsequent influence, changing to an item-then-price strategy seems a small price to pay.

Focusing on the order in which you present items might even apply in situations where, rather than selling a product or service, you are selling yourself. For example, this research would suggest that, rather than highlighting the number of years' experience on your resume followed by a list of accomplishments in that time, it might be more productive to present all your accomplishments first before mentioning the amount of time you served (e.g., "23 major projects in 2.5 years on the job"). Similarly, a new graduate might capture potential employers' attention to their academic achievements more effectively in their cover letter by pointing out they successfully completed 37 classes in 3.5 years in college rather than the other way round. While we would never claim that this small change alone will be your key to getting into the C-Suite, given the costless nature of this strategy it is another small change that, in the context of a crowded marketplace, could help make a difference.

## CHAPTER 39

# What SMALL BIG could end up getting you a lot more for much less?

Whether you are looking to improve the effectiveness of your communication in your personal life or in your professional life, the purpose of this book is to demonstrate, with scientific evidence, how making small changes in your approach can lead to big differences in how successful an influencer and persuader you are.

For example, imagine that you run a small business and you find yourself having to deal with an increasingly crowded marketplace where endless arrays of competitors are also vying for your customers' attention. In such a competitive environment it is clear that going the extra mile and offering a little more to your customers than your competitors do makes good sense. Adding an extra incentive of a bonus feature to your product or proposition could be the SMALL BIG that puts your business on the winning side, rather than the losing one.

But are there situations where adding extra information, additional incentives, or bonus features not only fails to strengthen your case but actually weakens it?

Or, put another way: Are there occasions when *more is less?*

Behavioural scientists Kimberlee Weaver, Stephen Garcia, and Norbert Schwarz thought that people tend to believe that offering extra features and information will strengthen their persuasion appeals largely due to the "additive" effect each extra feature brings. However, they also believed that people who evaluate their proposals will fail to appreciate these extras because—rather than providing an *additional* effect—they see them as providing an "averaging" effect instead. Rather like when you add warm water to hot water you end up with a more moderate temperature, sometimes attempts to clinch a deal by adding extra features to an already strong proposal can lead to a reduction in the overall attractiveness of your proposal.

To test their ideas the researchers set up a series of experiments including one in which study participants were assigned to either a presenter role or a purchaser role. Those in the presenter role were provided with two MP3 packages. Package one was in iPod touch that came with a choice of cover. Package two was exactly the same but this came with the added benefit of a free music download. Presenters were then asked to choose which package they considered to be the most valuable—in other words, which package they would offer to the potential purchasers. Those in the purchaser group were asked to imagine that they were looking to purchase an MP3 player for a friend; after being told about each of the two IPod touch packages, they were asked how much they would be willing to pay for each.

The overwhelming majority of presenters (92 percent) chose to offer the package that included the additional free music download. Interestingly, though, the purchaser group was willing to pay *less* for the iPod and cover package when it came bundled with the extra free song download than when than when no free song download was offered. Paradoxically, adding a music download to the package in an attempt to increase its value counter-intuitively cheapened it in the eyes of many purchasers.

In another experiment participants playing the role of customers searching for accommodation on a well-known travel website were asked how much, on average, they would be willing to pay to stay in a hotel with a five-star-rated pool. When those customers came to learn that the hotel also had a three-star-rated restaurant the amount they were willing to pay dropped by some 15 percent. Interestingly, almost three-quarters of another group of participants that played the role of the hotel owner wrongly predicted that adding the restaurant to their advertisement would allow them to command a higher average rate when in fact the opposite was true.*

***

Across a range of studies the researchers uncovered a consistent pattern. Sellers believed that spending more money and adding features to their already-strong propositions would strengthen their offers. Yet on each occasion adding an extra feature actually cheapened the overall proposition, resulting in customers saying they would pay less.

Now some of you may be thinking this is all very well for folks who sell products and services like iPods and hotel rooms, but does this effect extend to other types of influence challenges? For example, what if your challenge is to sell ideas rather than products?

It turns out the researchers thought of that too.

Let's imagine that you have taken a job at your local city council offices with the responsibility for reducing littering in the city's streets. Suppose further that part of your responsibility is to propose one of two penalty options for offenders who are caught littering. Which do you think you'd be more likely to recommend?

---

*Although the researchers didn't test this explicitly, customers likely would have paid more had the restaurant been rated five stars, since the average would have remained the same.

**Proposal A:** a $750.00 fine for those caught littering

Or

**Proposal B:** $750.00 fine + 2 hours of community service for those caught littering.

The researchers asked a number of government employees this exact question, finding that 86 percent recommended Proposal B even though a separate group of individuals evaluating the consequences rated the $750 fine + 2 hours of community service as *less* severe than a $750 fine alone! In this example, adding an extra *negative* feature to an already unattractive consequence made it slightly more attractive.

So why does this disparity between those presenting a proposal and those evaluating a proposal occur?

Weaver and her colleagues concluded that when constructing a persuasive appeal persuaders have a tendency to focus on each individual component of their offer, which leads them to take a piecemeal processing approach when they judge it. Evaluators, on the other hand, are more likely to process a persuasive appeal more holistically, focusing on the overall proposition.

So is the recommendation here simply for you to *not* provide extra information or features when making a case? Certainly not.

Instead the recommendations is to adopt the best parts of both of these strategies. Rather than investing additional resources to add a small extra feature for *every* customer, the advice here is to make a small shift by investing the same amount in a more significant feature for *fewer* selected customers. Doing so affords you two potential benefits.

First, you avoid wasting resources providing extra benefit that, as in the case of adding warm water to hot, might only serve to reduce the temperature of your overall offer. Second, you bring to bear the principle of reciprocity by providing customized, personalized, and significant additional benefits targeted to your most cherished customers.

## CHAPTER 40

# How could the SMALL act of unit-asking make a BIG difference to your appeals?

Imagine that you have an upcoming business trip. Recognizing that you'll have a couple of hours on the flight to catch up on some reading, you decide to pop down to your local bookstore to look for an interesting read. As you browse through the business bestseller lists you notice an interesting-looking book that claims to provide readers with over 50 ways to become a more effective and influential communicator. Given that the purpose of your trip is to meet a new client who you know will need a lot of convincing, you think that access to more than 50 persuasion strategies seems like something that will be really helpful to you. You decide to purchase the book.

Approaching the counter to pay, you notice that the price tag on the book is missing and, explaining that the store's computers are down, the store owner suggests that you simply pay what you think the book is worth. Would you be willing to pay more for this book of 52 insights if you first thought about how much you would be willing to pay for just 1 insight?

Behavioral scientists believe that the answer to this question is a clear yes. Interestingly, this seemingly trivial act of asking someone to first think about a smaller, individualized element of a request can make a big difference when it comes to getting them to say yes to subsequent and much larger elements of the request, too. This small BIG strategy, known as *unit-asking*, has potentially many uses beyond simply determining how much you are willing to pay for a book (regardless of how great it is).

By way of an example let's focus for a few moments on how a charity might use this small BIG strategy to increase donations to its cause. A common challenge that fundraisers have is that potential donors will often be insensitive to the number of people in need of help. As a result they will often donate similar amounts of money regardless of whether the true number in need is one person, hundreds, or even thousands of people. Researchers Christopher Hsee, Jiao Zhang, Zoe Lu, and Fei Xu thought that donors would contribute more to a campaign if they were asked first to indicate a hypothetical amount they would be willing to donate to help one victim.

In one of their studies, Hsee and his colleagues arranged for 800 employees working in a mid-sized Chinese company to receive an email from their employer encouraging them to take part in a fundraising program designed to help 40 students from low-income families. Those who were willing to help were asked to make their donation within one week of receiving the email message via a specific website that had been set up to receive their gifts. Three hundred and twenty employees responded and visited the website. However unbeknownst to them, half of them were directed to a standard website while the other half were directed to a "unit-asking" version of the website.

The employees who visited the standard website read the following:

> Think about these 40 students. How much are you willing to donate to help these 40 students? Please enter the amount of money you decide and agree to donate: ___ Yuan.

After entering their chosen donation amount on-screen, the employees were then given the option to revise their donation amount or to submit it.

The unit-asking version of the website was identical to the standard one but with an important difference. Before the employees were asked how much they would be willing to donate for all 40 students, they were first asked to think hypothetically about their willingness to help just one student.

Specifically the unit-asking website stated

Before deciding how much to donate to help these 40 students, please first think about one such student and answer a hypothetical question: How much would you donate to help this one student? Please indicate the amount here: _____ Yuan.

After respondents typed the amount they would hypothetically donate to one student, they were then asked how much they would be willing to donate for all 40.

This simple act of unit-asking had a significant impact on donations. Donors in the standard website group gave an average of 315 yuan (around US $50), but those in the unit-asking group donated an average of 600 yuan (over $95). Posing a unit-asking question first was the small BIG that increased donations by 90 percent.

So far so good. But isn't there a potential downside to the strategy? For example, could the posing of the unit-asking question reduce the overall percentage of visitors who leave a donation because some people would object to being asked this odd question? The researchers considered this possibility and were able to report that the extra question had no significant impact on the overall number of visitors who went on to donate.

For fundraisers the advice seems pretty clear. When

constructing an appeal, it can be tempting to communicate to potential donors the scale of the problem you are trying to deal with by highlighting the large number of people in need. However, doing that may actually reduce rather than increase the average contribution to your cause. Instead it is beneficial for you to direct potential donors' attention to what amount they might be willing to give to just one individual in need before requesting a pledge for the larger number.

Beyond fundraising and charitable appeals there are other areas where the small BIG of unit-asking could lead to desirable outcomes. Managers trying to increase their annual budget for travel might be more successful at pitching for the funds needed to accomplish their goals by first asking their department heads to consider how much they would fund for a single trip. Similarly, educators who lobby parents and supporters for much-needed school books might inquire about their willingness to support the reading needs of one child before broadening the appeal to the whole classroom. An eBayer might garner higher bids when selling goods online that come in sets (e.g., glassware, box-set DVDs, and luggage) if they pose the question "How much would you be willing to pay for just one?" alongside their product descriptions.

It is important to recognize, however, that despite there being many potential contexts for deploying this unit-asking strategy, there is one specific situation in which this approach is likely to be limited—when the broader target numbers are especially large. For example, Hsee and his colleagues suggest in situations where a charitable campaign is seeking to help tens of thousands of needy folks that the act of unit-asking is unlikely to have an effect due to people's tendency to encode large numbers such as tens of thousands as simply "a lot."

Does this mean that all is lost in circumstances where fundraisers are looking to persuade donors to contribute to campaigns in which many thousands of people require help? Certainly not. But it does require fundraisers to adopt a different strategy: a strategy, like all the others in this book, that requires just a small shift in emphasis, and one that we take a closer look at in the next chapter.

CHAPTER 41

# Why would highlighting identifiable features be the SMALL BIG that boosts your campaign efforts?

On 13 March 2002 an Indonesian tanker caught fire some 600 miles off the coast of Honolulu killing one crew member and wiping out all power and communications aboard the ship. It would be another three weeks before a passing cruise ship spotted a distress signal and, pulling alongside, rescued the captain and ten surviving crew members.

It remains unclear why the captain's dog, a two-year-old terrier crossbreed called Forgea, was left behind during the rescue, but a remark made by one of the cruise ship passengers during a news channel interview that she thought she saw a dog left behind sparked a rescue mission. The operation, which was coordinated by the American Marine Corps, lasted 16 days and cost $48,000, mostly financed by a fundraising campaign launched by a local charity called the Hawaiian Humane Society. Given that the per head cost of rescuing the crew averaged less than half the sum for saving the dog, it might be worth asking which features of the fundraising campaign were responsible for persuading Hawaiians to raise such a remarkable sum of money to save one animal. More broadly, it is also worth asking whether these same lessons apply not only to fundraising and charitable appeals, but to other influence and persuasion challenges.

196

Previous research has shown that one way fundraising organizations can influence both the number of donors that contribute to a campaign and the generosity of those donors is to draw audience attention to a specific feature of an identified victim that *individualizes* him or her—such as the person's age, gender, or even hair color. Making these small but crucial details available early on in a communication serves to focus attention on the individual life at stake. This, in turn, increases the value people place on that life compared to when that same victim is presented as abstract, anonymous, or part of a larger group. For example, one study looking at the medical decisions made by physicians found that when a photograph of a patient was included on their CT scan, doctors recommended more caring and attentive treatment because it enabled them to focus on the patient as an identifiable individual rather than as part of a group of patients.

The idea that people feel more generous when their attention is drawn to a victim that is presented as both an individual and identifiable might go some way in explaining the extraordinary flood of donations to save Forgea. As the only canine on board a ship full of sailors, she was certainly identifiable. Reports describing her as a white terrier mixed breed that enjoyed eating pizza and who weighed in at 40 pounds served to present her as an individual too—albeit a rather hefty one.

Accordingly, a simple change that anyone can make when seeking the support of others could be to highlight, early on, small, specific, and important features that both identify and individualize the beneficiaries of their campaign. Beyond the clear implications for charities, perhaps managers at budget negotiation time could, rather than simply pointing to meaningless numbers on a spreadsheet, instead show images that identify and individualize the people in their teams. "This is Mary, our head analyst, who together with Jim and Lindsay and their teams need a system upgrade this year, which accounts for X percent of the increase in the budget I am submitting."

Such appeals could be advanced even more by making an additional small change aligned with another insight from persuasion science. Social scientists Cynthia Cryder, George Loewnstein, and Richard Scheines hypothesized that in addition to highlighting an "identified individual," a campaign could be further boosted by stressing an "identified intervention."

In one of their experiments participants were randomly assigned to three groups and presented with an online scenario about donating to Oxfam. In a "general charity condition," participants read:

> Oxfam International is one of the most effective aid organizations in the world. Oxfam provides a broad range of humanitarian aid to people across the globe. If you were asked to donate to Oxfam, how much would you give?

In a second condition, "charity details—high impact," they read the same message but with one addition:

> One example of how Oxfam uses funds is by providing individuals with access to clean water.

Finally, participants in a "charity details—low impact" condition read the same sentence except the word "clean" was changed to "bottled" because pre-tests had shown that "clean" water was perceived to create more impact than "bottled" water.

While the wording changes made across the appeals could be considered tiny, the impact on donations was anything but tiny. Compared to participants in the "general charity condition," who indicated they would donate an average of $7.50, participants in the "charity details—high impact" group (who were furnished with information about how the money would be used) gave 37 percent more. That's an impressive uplift for such a small change. Thus, you would be well advised to supplement your appeals for extra resources—regardless of whether for information, time, money, or even people—by adding an identifiable intervention to your proposal.

Similarly the manager seeking extra budget for a systems upgrade would be advised to point out to budget holders the specific impact that providing extra resources to Mary and her team would have. But what kinds of specific impact should one point toward?

For a potential answer let's take a closer look at the Cryder, Loewnstein, and Scheines study, specifically at the participants in the charity details–low impact condition who were told they were contributing toward bottled, rather than clean, water. You probably won't be surprised to learn that they donated less than those told they were contributing toward clean water. But you may well be surprised to learn that they also gave less than those in the general charity condition who weren't given any additional information at all.

The reason is that when attempting to boost appeals for more resources, details about interventions only matter to the extent that they promote a perceived impact. In the Oxfam example it is easy to see why potential donors would believe that providing bottled water would have much less of a perceived impact than providing clean water—so much so that it actually led to donations at an even lower level than when the information wasn't given in the first place.

This insight calls into focus a related yet still all-too-common trap that communicators fall into. When highlighting the impact of the extra resources that they are requesting, they often make the mistake of promoting the effect the resources will have on themselves rather than the perceived impact they will have on those who actually provide the resources. For example, it is easy to see how the manager pitching for extra resources to finance a system upgrade might focus on the actual impact it will have on *her team's* ability to deliver improved services—rather than the perceived impact those improved services will have on the rest of the organization.

Therefore, whenever you find yourself in a situation where you need to persuade others to give up resources to help you achieve a goal, these small BIGs demonstrate that you should focus your audience's attention on the identifying features of both the entity and the intervention involved.

## CHAPTER 42

# What SMALL BIG can ensure that your costs are not opportunities lost?

Whether you're persuading customers to buy your products, clients to hire your advisory services, or colleagues to support your new initiatives, if you're like most people, you'll agree that the job tends to be a whole lot easier not only when you have a strong case to make, but also when the case you are making shows a clear price advantage, too.

But sometimes, even when we have the best combination of product and price, our attempts still fail. There are several potential reasons why this occurs, but one of the more important ones concerns a common error that people in an advantageous position often make. Fortunately, communicators who are aware of this error not only are in a better position to avoid it, but can also—by making a small change to their message—significantly increase their advantage over rival communicators at the same time.

The common error we are talking about is a tendency for people to fail to consider what economists call the "opportunity cost" of a decision. The opportunity cost of a decision is simply the potential direct benefits people could have received had they made an alternative choice. For example, imagine that you decide to go to the gym on the way to work tomorrow morning. The opportunity cost of that decision is what you will give up—in this case, an extra hour snoozing in bed. When it comes to persuasion, the mistake often made by communicators is to assume that their targets of influence (e.g., the people whom they are trying to persuade) will automatically consider their own opportunity costs when making decisions. For example, imagine that you are selling a product that is not only of a good standard, but also less costly than a similar product sold by a competitor. As the seller, it is easy to assume that your potential customers will instantly recognize the savings they can make and, by appropriately weighing the cost differential, decide that your option is the one they should choose.

But research conducted by consumer behavior researcher Shane Frederick and his colleagues suggests that people don't weigh this information nearly as much as you would expect them to. And when that happens what you might consider to be your biggest competitive advantage can potentially turn out to be a nonfactor if you fail to take small steps to be more proactive in your approach.

On the face of things, it sounds obvious that decision makers would strongly consider factors like the opportunity costs of choosing Option A over the less expensive Option B. It seems like a no-brainer that when making a decision, people would realize that spending $500 more on Option A means that they won't have that $500 to spend on other opportunities. Yet Frederick and his colleagues believed that, especially when people are overloaded with too many choices and decisions, they don't think much about this. Their studies suggest a simple yet often overlooked solution to the potential problem: Give decision makers a little help by making the trade-off in cost a little more explicit with some gentle prodding.

In one of their studies participants were randomly assigned to one of two groups and offered the chance to purchase a DVD for $14.99. One group was presented with the choice to either

"Buy the DVD" or "Not buy the DVD." However the second group was presented with a choice to either "Buy the DVD" or "Keep the $14.99 for other purchases." Despite the fact that the two descriptions are equivalent—after all, "not buying" implies keeping the money for other purchases—this small change led to a big difference, with purchase rates in the second group dropping from 75 percent to 55 percent.

The authors of the research noted that the furniture manufacturer and retailer IKEA used this strategy brilliantly in an advertising campaign in Singapore. In one advertisement, the left pane featured an unhappy woman standing by a fancy-looking cabinet containing only a single pair of shoes. The caption underneath read, "Customized cabinet $1,670 + 1 pair of shoes $30 = $1,700." In contrast, the right pane of the ad featured a woman in front of a less ornate IKEA cabinet that was filled to the brim with shoes. The caption underneath showed that the cabinet's price ($245) plus the price of 48 pairs of shoes ($1,440) was still less than the $1,700 from the left pane.

It is interesting to note that in the IKEA ad example the savings were used to purchase products related to the featured item (i.e., shoes and shoe-storing furniture). However, Frederick and his colleagues found that this doesn't always have to be the case.

In another experiment, participants were asked to choose between two cell phones, with the higher-quality option costing $20 more. However, a little earlier, half of the participants had been asked to think about items—any items—they could buy for about $20. It turns out these participants were about 50 percent more likely to choose the less expensive cell phone than those who were not asked explicitly to think about what they could buy with $20.

Therefore one small change that every communicator can make that could lead to a big difference in their message's effectiveness is to be explicit about the advantages their offer will garner in addition to the offer itself. A politician describing how her new policy will save the average household $250 a year might go on to describe the sorts of things that a family might be able to do with the extra cash, such as a family leisure trip, an extra boost to the college fund, or simply a little bit extra for a rainy day. Similarly an IT consultant wishing to persuade a client of the merits of his favorably priced software system could bolster that already strong position by illustrating related examples of what the savings in time and money could be used for.

A sales manager who asks her team to consider how they would spend next quarter's sales bonus should they achieve their goal might be engaging a small BIG that leads to an increased sales performance—especially if those spending plans are then made public on the team's bulletin board.

Adopting small BIGs that make opportunity costs more salient could benefit your retirement plans, too. One of us has a friend who, like many couples with children, faces the continual trade-off between spending today vs. saving for an earlier and potentially more comfortable retirement. Their small BIG solution is to create a unit of spending called "retire one week early." When this couple contemplates expensive decisions, they compare the cost of the decision to the opportunity cost of retiring a few weeks earlier. Not long ago they told us that friends of theirs had recently moved to a more expensive house, prompting them to consider doing the same. However, when it became obvious that if they were to move the cost would be the equivalent of them having to retire four years *later* than their target, it quickly became evident to them that it was something they didn't want to do.

Of course, it is also important to keep in mind that the opportunities you highlight with your savings should be good ones. The authors point to one anti-war website that described the cost of the war in Iraq (which at the time had reached an estimated $300 billion for the United States) as "the loss of nine Twinkies per American per day for a year." In this context it seems likely that however well-intentioned the message, the peace advocates may have unwittingly become their own worst enemy.

However ill-advised this attempt was, there is an important underlying message that can serve anyone whose products, propositions, and policies carry a high price. Instead of framing the opportunity costs as attractive and important, frame them as unattractive or unimportant. The diamond mining and trading company De Beers offered a wonderful example in a recent advertisement depicting a photograph of two large diamond earrings. The tagline?

"Redo the kitchen *next* year."

## CHAPTER 43

# What SMALL BIG can help to motivate others (and yourself) to complete tasks?

I magine that one day you and a friend meet for coffee. After you order and pay for your drinks, the barista hands you a loyalty card and explains that each time you buy a cup of coffee they will stamp your card. Once you have collected ten stamps you can claim a free cup of coffee. You take the card from the barista and notice that she has already stamped your card *twice* to get you on your way toward that free cup of coffee.

The progress you have now made toward your free cup of coffee could be framed in one of two ways. Either you are 20 percent of the way toward achieving that free cup of coffee or you have 80 percent remaining. But which is more likely to motivate you to complete the task?

It turns out the answer isn't relevant just to a coffee shop owner looking to influence her customers to be more loyal, but to anyone whose challenge requires them to persuade others (and even themselves) to complete tasks. (And by the way, before you continue reading, you should know that you have already completed 10 percent of this particular chapter of *The small BIG.*)

Persuasion researchers Minjung Koo and Ayelet Fishbach thought that an individual's motivation to complete a task could be improved by making a small change in where they focused their attention. They hypothesized that, at the begining of a task, getting individuals to concentrate on the smaller amount of progress they had already made toward a goal would be more motivating than focusing on the larger amount of effort that remained.

In order to test their ideas, Koo and Fishbach conducted a fascinating series of studies, including one in a popular sushi restaurant. Over a period of four months some 900 regular customers were enrolled in a loyalty program where they would receive a free lunch of their choice after purchasing ten lunches. Half the customers in the study were given a blank card and were told that a sushi-shaped stamp would be added to their card each time they bought lunch. By providing a stamp for each purchase, a customer's attention was directed to the progress they were making toward their end goal. Let's call these customers the "progress *accumulated*" group.

The other half of the customers were given a card that was already printed with ten sushi-shaped stamps on it. Each time these folks bought a lunch, instead of having a stamp added, a stamp was removed with a hole puncher. As a result, the attention of these customers was focused on how much progress remained before they received their free lunch. We'll call these customers the "progress *remaining*" group.

At this point we should highlight the fact that because this study was carried out in a working restaurant there were a range of different transactions. For example, a customer who just bought lunch for themselves would get one stamp added or taken away on their loyalty card, meaning that they made only a little bit of progress toward their free lunch. But a customer who bought lunch for themselves and a group of friends or business associates would receive multiple stamps (or have multiple stamps removed from their loyalty card) meaning they made lots of progress toward theirs.

Analyzing the results, the researchers found that those customers who made only a little bit of initial progress by buying lunch just for themselves or a small number of other people were much more likely to return to the restaurant in the "progress accumulated" condition. However the reverse was true for customers who made a lot of initial progress—those customers were more likely to return if their attention was focused on the "progress remaining" to get the free lunch.

Why the difference? Because in both cases customers were more motivated to complete the goal when their focus was directed to the smaller number—whether that small number concerned the progress already made (you're 30 percent of the way to a free lunch) or the effort that remained (you've only 30 percent to go).

Koo and Fishbach coined the phrase "small-area hypothesis" for this concept.

So the implication is clear. Whether your goal is to increase the success of your company's customer loyalty program or simply to encourage others (or even yourself) to be more motivated to complete a task, this study suggests that you can increase the chances of success by, in the early stages, having your audience (or yourself) focus on the small amount of *progress* that has already been made rather than on the larger amount that remains.

One reason for this is because in the early stages of a task, focusing on the smaller number appeals to the human desire to behave as efficiently as possible. An action that moves someone from 20 percent completion of a task to 40 percent completion has doubled their progress—which seems like a very efficient action indeed. Contrast that with moving from 60 percent completion to 80 percent, which, although the same 20 percent difference, represents progress of just a quarter of the total completed.

As a result, a manager or supervisor, keen to keep her staff motivated to reach a particular sales goal or performance target, might find that their early motivation can be maintained by providing feedback on the progress that her team members have already made by telling her staff, "We're only one week into the new quarter and you've already achieved 15 percent of your quarterly target," rather than "We've made a great start in our first week and now we've got 85 percent of the way to go."

Similarly a person keen to motivate himself to regularly save a little spare cash to buy a new high-definition TV, or a couple looking to pay off a credit card or personal loan, could improve their commitment to their financial plans by focusing on the small but important progress they have already made toward their goals. Banks and financial societies might even help their customers by signaling the progress they have made toward a savings or repayment plan on their statements and online banking pages, in much the same way that LinkedIn signals the progress people have made toward completing their online profile.

But remember the customers in the sushi restaurant who initially bought lots of lunches, meaning they immediately accumulated stamps that pushed them much nearer to the completion of the loyalty card? In their case the progress remaining was actually smaller than the progress accumulated. Remember too that they were much more likely to complete the task when their attention was focussed on the smaller effort remaining.

This means that a small shift needs to be made when the halfway mark of any goal is reached. Once the halfway mark is passed, people's motivation to complete a task will typically be higher when feedback is shifted to the smaller amount of effort *remaining*. So messages like "You only have 20 percent left to achieve your goal" will likely be more effective than "You are 80 percent of the way to achieving your goal."

So with just 20 percent of this chapter left for you to read, now might be a good time to provide some practical examples of how this small shift in focus could lead to potentially big differences in your influence and persuasion attempts!

From airlines and hotels to coffee shops and cosmetics retailers, many businesses operate customer reward programs that have a feedback mechanism already built in, so that their customers know how much progress they are making toward that flight upgrade, free night, or, in the case of coffeehouses, their next free double chocolate mocha! The small-area hypothesis suggests that regardless of where a particular customer is on that reward journey, feedback should always focus on the small area regardless of whether it is progress made or effort remaining. Frequent flyer statements should highlight the miles earned toward an upgrade up until the halfway point and then shift to highlighting miles remaining to reach the reward. Baristas should verbally signal to customers the small progress made or the small effort remaining when stamping customers' coffee cards.

Similarly, those involved in coaching and training others should be careful to frame their feedback and recommendations in a way that highlights the smaller area of attainment achieved or remaining. Managers and supervisors looking to influence and persuade staff to improve their skills might include such small-area signals on employees' personal development plans. One way this could be done would be to add the percentage of progress an employee has made toward achieving a particular objective on their development plan, making sure to switch at the halfway point from progress made to progress remaining. This small change increases the chances that an employee's attention will be focused on the smaller area, which could lead to big differences in their performance.

And when it comes to motivating yourself to get through that 60-minute Spinning class or next weekend's 10K run, a focus on the time or distance endured in the early stages before transferring to the time or distance remaining toward the end could help get you through such challenges. Alternatively, to add momentum to your personal weight-loss program (or a month-long smoking abstinence), emphasize the weight you've already lost (or days without a cigarette) in the early stages before directing attention to weight still needed to be lost (or smoke-free days left) to reach your desired goal.

## CHAPTER 44

# What SMALL BIG can lead to greater customer loyalty?

The online wine store yesmywine.com has a rather interesting rewards program. When customers purchase wine from a specific country they are given a "Country Medal." Customers who collect 12 different medals over the course of a year are rewarded with a large bonus. However there is a catch. In order to claim their reward, customers must collect the medals in a specific sequence that is mandated by the wine store. For example, customers might be required to purchase, say, a bottle of French wine in January, an Australian wine in February, an Italian wine in March, and so on over the course of a year, rather than simply being told to purchase 12 bottles from the 12 different countries in an order of their choosing.

Considering that the actual number of purchases required never changes (it is always 12 bottles) this rewards program seems overly rigid. One would think that compared to standard loyalty programs, an oddly restrictive program such as this one would be less likely to attract customers to enroll. After all, when it comes to persuading people to complete tasks, especially those that require multiple steps and actions (or purchases in the case of a loyalty program), most people report preferring flexibility and the removal of unnecessary barriers.

So why would a company, which we assume wants to attract more customers and promote long-term loyalty, design a program that seemingly goes against the grain of what most people would sign up for? It turns out that yesmywine.com has recognized something counter-intuitive. Although people report a preference for flexibility when achieving goals and objectives, *rigidity can have a surprisingly positive influence on whether those goals are completed.*

When deciding whether to pursue a particular goal or objective, people will typically consider two things—its value and how realistically attainable it is. For example, a business development team tasked with winning a significant and strategically important new client needs to assess not only the value of that new client but also their realistic chances of securing them. Similarly it's not enough for an individual who wishes to learn a new skill or retrain for a new job to simply imagine how different her life will be if she does. She will also need to consider the actual steps and actions she will need to take in order to achieve her goals.

Given that achievement of a goal requires not only its adoption but also its pursuit, are there any situations when something that persuades us to pursue a goal then gets in our way when it comes to achieving that same goal? For example, in the case of the online wine store, the flexibility to make wine purchases in any order could be seen as more attractive than requiring customers to purchase wines in a specific sequence. As a result, more customers could be persuaded to enroll in the rewards program. But once they have enrolled, does the flexibility that attracted them to the program actually *reduce* their motivation to complete the purchases required to achieve the reward they signed up for in the first place?

Behavioral scientists Liyan Jin, Szu-chi Huang, and Ying Zhang thought that more people would sign up for a goal requiring them to complete multiple actions if they were able to choose the order in which they completed those actions as compared to people who had the order prescribed to them, but that once the process of achieving the goal began, those given the flexibility would be less likely to complete the goal than those who were not.

To test their idea, 800 customers at a busy city center yogurt store were offered a reward card entitling them to a free yogurt after six standard purchases. Half the cards required the purchase of six different flavors of yogurt in any order. The other half required customers to purchase six different flavors in the prescribed order of banana–apple–strawberry–orange–mango–grape. Additionally, half the cards required a customer to return the next day to activate the card with the other half being told that the card had already been activated. These last two conditions were important because they enabled the researchers to measure a customer's motivation to start the task by requiring them to make a separate return trip.

Consistent with their initial hypothesis, those customers given a reward card that allowed them to purchase the six flavors of yogurt in a flexible order were significantly more likely to activate their card than those told they had to purchase in a fixed sequence (30 percent vs. 12 percent). Interestingly, though, when it came to completion rates, the opposite was true. Customers given reward cards that required a fixed sequence of purchases were significantly more likely to make all the required purchases.

But why?

One likely reason is that a predetermined sequence eliminates, or at least reduces, the number of unnecessary "decision points" that can arise when people pursue a plan. And one thing that today's information-overloaded citizens appreciate is the need to make fewer, not more, decisions. In additional studies, Jin and colleagues found evidence to support this idea:

People who followed a fixed sequence typically reported that limiting the choices made during the pursuit of a goal actually made the goal (a) more likely to be achieved and (b) feel easier in the process.

So far, so good, but hold on a minute. Although those customers given a rigid purchase sequence were more likely to make the purchases required to get their free yogurt, fewer of them signed up for the rewards program in the first place. So if a rigid structure increases people's likelihood to complete a goal but reduces uptake rates in the first place, what's the overall net effect? The researchers looked at this, too. The answer, as often happens in persuasion science, is that it depends on the context.

In situations where the choice being made is relatively simple and the motivation to achieve the task is quite strong, a flexible rather than fixed sequence typically leads to better goal achievement. But where the change that is required is harder or where motivation levels might be lower, creating a rigid sequence and structure should be more effective at increasing completion levels.

This research has obvious implications for how companies should design their customer loyalty and rewards programs. But there are a number of other applications as well. Imagine a manager who wants colleagues to adopt a new initiative. Before structuring the required actions in a flexible or lock-step sequence, the manager needs to ask herself a *small* question with big potential consequences: "Is my major problem here likely to be getting buy-in or follow-through?" If the answer is that the main difficulty will be getting colleagues on board in the first place, the implication is clear—make the sequence of required steps as flexible as is practicable and emphasize that flexibility when announcing the initiative.

But, if the bigger problem will arise at the execution phase, the implication is equally clear though entirely different—give the roll-out sequence a very structured order and emphasize how, once in place, the program will proceed in a straightforward, uncomplicated fashion.

The idea that a structured order can help people to complete certain goals and programs might prove to be a useful insight to healthcare companies who face the challenge of persuading people to complete courses of medicines they have been prescribed. The findings from this study suggest that changing the pills in blister packs from a single color to multiple colors and setting out clear instructions to users about which pill to take at a specific time could be beneficial to both patients and healthcare professionals. For example, patients could be instructed to take white tablets for the first three days of treatment, blue tablets for the next three days, and then complete the course by taking red tablets. Although nothing would change about the active ingredients of the pharmaceutical itself, the structure set out for taking the medicine could be a small change that potentially leads to an increase in patient compliance.

In a similar vein, retailers and manufacturers of self-assembly products, such as furniture, might find some customers more likely to follow recommended assembly instructions if they color-code each stage of the construction process, explicitly pointing out the order in which tasks should be carried out. Not only could this small change potentially make assembly easier, in some cases it might save a few relationships as well.

And when it comes to motivating yourself to learn a new skill—especially if it is a difficult one or you're in a situation where there are lots of other distractions in your life—this rigid approach, while much less attractive at the outset, might make the difference when it comes to achieving the ukulele skills that will ensure your inclusion in that folk band you've always dreamed of joining.

## CHAPTER 45

# How could a SMALL BIG result in 1 + 1 getting you more than 2?

As any good economist will tell you, people respond to incentives. But as a behavioral psychologist will also point out, an individual's response to incentives may be influenced as much by the context in which the incentive is presented as by what's actually being offered. For example, people are generally more persuaded by the thought of losing something than the thought of gaining that exact same thing. In the arena of loss versus gain, what is the same economically becomes very different psychologically.

Timing can provide an important context, too. Studies have shown our tendency to live for today at the expense of tomorrow. Offered a choice between $20 today and $21 tomorrow, most people will take the money now. Change the context, though—$20 seven days from now or $21 in eight days—and more people will wait the extra day for the bigger reward and, in doing so, demonstrate how fascinatingly inconsistent human decisions and behavior can sometimes be.

So when it comes to using incentives to influence behaviors, the contextual framing can matter an awful lot. According to one study it appears that a seemingly small and inconsequential change, such as separating rewards into different categories, can increase people's motivation to acquire them—even if the categories are meaningless.

Behavioral scientists Scott Wiltermuth and Francesca Gino believed that people's motivation to achieve a reward could be affected by the category in which the reward was placed. In one of their studies, participants were asked to complete a simple ten-minute writing task in exchange for a reward. The possible rewards consisted of a mix of inexpensive items displayed in two large plastic containers from which participants could choose one reward. But all participants were told that if they (voluntarily) chose to complete a second 10-minute task—therefore working a total of 20 minutes—they could choose a second item from the available rewards.

Unbeknownst to the participants, they had been randomly assigned to one of two groups, and there was one important difference in the information given to the two groups. The first group was told that if they completed the additional writing task, they could take their second reward from any of the containers. In contrast, the second group was told that if they completed the additional task, the two rewards they selected would have to come from different containers, because the containers held "two categories of rewards."

Remarkably, despite the fact that all the participants clearly saw that the two containers contained the same mix of items, those in the second group were *three times more* motivated to complete the additional task than were those in the first group. Perhaps even more surprising was the fact that the enjoyment of the writing tasks was significantly higher among the participants who were told they would be choosing from two categories rather than one.

So why did the prospect of receiving rewards from two categories energize people to a greater extent than did the prospect of receiving the same number and value of rewards from only one category? And why were they happier too?

According to Wiltermuth and Gino, dividing the rewards into categories (even meaningless ones) made people feel that they would be "losing out" on something if they didn't complete the additional task. Thus, when seeking to influence people to complete tasks by offering incentives or rewards, separating those incentives or rewards into different categories can, without increasing their economic value, increase their *psychological* value because of people's aversion to missing out on something.

These findings could provide useful insights to anyone who has an interest in, or a responsibility for, motivating others through the use of incentives. For example, a sales manager tasked with motivating employees through a new sales incentive or bonus program could optimize the program by offering rewards that fall into two distinct categories and then allow his team access to the second category of rewards only after they have earned one from the first. Not only would such an arrangement encourage employees to expend the effort to attain both types of rewards, it might even lead them to enjoy those efforts more in the bargain.

This recategorization effect could even help those in financial difficulties. People with multiple debts typically have a tendency to pay off their smaller debts first because it understandably provides a sense of progress toward financial freedom. Of course doing so often makes matters worse because the larger debts are simply accumulating more interest, deepening the pool of debt. Banks and financial houses could help by offering to split larger debts into two smaller ones, say Debt A and Debt B, which may not financially reduce the debtor's burden, but would at least psychologically reduce it. This small change, which would focus people's attention on a larger, more costly debt, could make for a big difference in reducing interest paid.

## CHAPTER 46

# How could a SMALL step back lead to a BIG leap forward?

The complexity of modern-day life can serve up some pretty challenging situations that even the most seasoned and experienced of people can find difficult to navigate. Fortunately—or unfortunately, depending on your point of view—answers to how to deal with that difficult customer or suggestions for tackling a knotty issue in the office are never that far away. They come in the form of a helpful colleague or coworker who appears only too pleased to pass on the benefit of their wisdom and experience to you.

But sometimes advice such as "You should sleep on it" and "Why not take a step back and view the issue from a distance?" while not lacking good intentions, may reflect the lack of a deeper understanding of your situation. This is primarily because your challenge tends to look very different to them because of their detached point of view. But before you completely dismiss their counsel as unhelpful or as largely generic, it might be worth considering the following: When it comes to thinking about solutions to problems, there is scientific evidence that points toward the benefits of consciously creating some physical distance from the problem at hand.

Perhaps of even greater interest is the finding that creating physical distance is not only instructive when it comes to solving problems and making decisions, it can also give us a distinct persuasive advantage. For example, especially in the early stages of proposals and presentations, asking potential customers to take a step back before they consider your products and services could actually make it easier for them to subsequently do business with you.

Researchers Manoj Thomas and Claire Tsai thought that the *physical distance* between a person and the challenge or problem that they faced could influence their perception of how easy or difficult overcoming that challenge or problem would be. In one set of experiments participants were asked to read out loud a series of words that appeared on a computer screen in front of them. On certain occasions some of the words that appeared on the screen were what the researchers described as "orthographically irregular non-words," which is scientific talk for a faux word that is made up and difficult to pronounce (e.g., "meunstah"). At other times participants were asked to read aloud non-words that were simple and easy to pronounce (e.g., "hension").

In an interesting twist, immediately before one of the difficult-to-pronounce non-words appeared on the screen, half the participants were instructed to lean toward the screen in order to reduce the physical distance between themselves and the non-word. The other half of the participants, however, were asked to lean back so that the distance between themselves and the non-word was actually increased.

Finally, after reading out each non-word, the study's participants were then asked to rate how difficult they found it to pronounce.

The results showed that when it came to reading out the difficult-to-pronounce non-words, those who were asked to lean back in their chairs reported finding the task *easier* than those who were asked to move toward the screen. In short the experiment neatly demonstrated that when facing a tricky task, simply taking a physical step back and viewing that task from a greater distance can prove to be useful in reducing your perception of how difficult that task actually is. So next time you're stuck on that Sudoku puzzle or you're struggling to make something meaningful from the wretched set of Scrabble tiles you've picked, taking a step back and looking at the challenge from a greater distance might be the small change that makes a big difference.

But what about situations when these challenge concerns something other than word pronunciation tasks or games of Scrabble? For example, imagine for a few moments that you are viewing a product that you are potentially interested in purchasing. Does the distance between you and that product have any influence over how easy the buying decision becomes?

To answer this question the researchers went on to conduct another series of experiments, this time asking participants to evaluate and choose from a range of electronic products that included items such as cameras and computers. Participants were shown a number of choices in a particular product range and given information that compared the features of each option reviewed. In order to closely reflect what often happens in real life, the comparisons between the different products were quite difficult to evaluate.

Additionally it was made clear to the participants that there were no obvious cost benefits that marked one particular product as a better purchase than another. Finally the researchers varied the distance from which the products were reviewed, with some participants reviewing them close up and others from a greater distance.

Immediately after reviewing the products, the participants were given a choice to either consider which product they liked best and purchase it there and then, or to defer their decision for another time.

Consistent with the word pronunciation tests, the results clearly showed that those who were told to take a step back and create some distance between themselves and the products found the evaluation task easier and, as a result, were significantly less likely to delay their purchasing decision. In contrast, those asked to compare their options from a closer distance were much more likely to delay their purchase decision.

In summary, here's the small BIG: A small change, brought about by increasing the physical distance from which a choice is viewed, makes a big difference in how quickly people make their purchase decisions. Put another way, complex product choices do appear to get a little easier when viewed from a greater distance.

The findings give us certain small, but potentially important, staging changes to consider when attempting to influence the decisions of others. Imagine for a few moments that you are pitching for a piece of business with a new client and that the solution your organization is offering is relatively complex but objectively the best of the available options. These studies suggest that the distance from which your proposal will be viewed could turn out to be quite important. Accordingly it will be important not only to carefully consider the content of your presentation, but also to pay close attention to the distance from which your content will be viewed. This might mean that instead of presenting directly from your laptop where the viewer may have to get much closer to the screen in order to see what you are proposing, it might be wiser to (a) arrange for your presentation to be projected against a bigger screen, even if you are presenting to a small audience of one or two people, or (b) invest in a big-screen laptop that will allow more distance between the screen and your audience.

Similarly, a teacher leading a lesson that contains relatively difficult subject matter such as math might find that her pupils' perceptions of the lesson's difficulty can be reduced if she arranges for a greater physical distance between the students and the material. One way this could be done would be to ask her students to work standing at a whiteboard or flipchart rather than sitting down with a writing pad or exercise book. Doing so would provide an environment where it is easier for her pupils to physically step back from the taxing problem she has set in front of them (rather than leaning back in their chairs or even getting up out of them and creating a disturbance).

Retail sales staffs who demonstrate products as part of a sales process might benefit from carefully considering the physical distance between themselves and their customers. For example, a salesperson in an electronics store who is demonstrating a range of cell phones might choose to retreat slightly to create a greater distance between themselves and the customer—especially at points when they are introducing relatively complex or technical product features to nonexpert customers.

All in all, these studies go some way to explaining how small changes to the physical distance from which information is viewed can make a big difference when it comes to influencing perceptions and easing decision making.

They might also go some way to explaining why, when agonizing over that knotty problem in the office, it's the smug colleague looking over your shoulder at your screen from a distance who always believes they can get to the answer quicker than you.

## CHAPTER 47

# How can you make BIG strides from others' SMALL stumbles?

A certain kind of awe is due to the turnaround artist who can turn bad into good—lemons into lemonade, straw into gold. Such accomplishments are especially impressive when the bad is some form of failure that gets transformed into consequent success. Note that the operative term here is *consequent*. We're not referring to the *subsequent* success occasionally brought about by perseverance, belligerence, or an attitude of "try, try, and try again." Rather we are talking about faults that become game-winners *precisely* because they were faulty.

There are a number of ways to make previous errors bear fruit. Some, such as reengineering a business model, eliminating system bugs, and finding new ways to navigate around unforeseen barriers, will require a substantial investment in time and resources. This is big stuff and often it will be crucial. But small things are important too. Surprisingly one of the easier ways to snatch victory from the jaws of defeat doesn't even require you to think about your past mistakes. Instead the advice is to make a small shift and think about the mistakes that *others* have made instead.

Charlie Munger is both brilliant and wise—attributes that yield big payouts. It is because of those conjoined traits that he is Warren Buffett's business partner and most trusted adviser within the investment firm of Berkshire Hathaway, which, since its inception in 1964, has been successful at levels never before seen in that industry. Mr. Munger was once asked to describe the steps he takes to ensure that any choice he makes is likely to be a sound one.

He replied simply, "I review my inanities list."

Mr. Munger keeps a file of foolishness…filled with the flops and the fatal fumbles that brought them forth. Rather than following the conventional wisdom of identifying and imitating the shrewd decisions that have led to business successes, as chronicled in such bestsellers as *Good to Great, In Search of Excellence,* and *Made to Last,* he chooses to spend his time identifying and avoiding the inane decisions that have led to others' business blunders.

So why might an activity that on the surface appears relatively small make for a potentially big difference—not just for Mr. Munger's and Berkshire Hathaway's decisions, but for yours as well?

One reason is that large-scale achievements can rarely be attributed to any lone factor. The foundation of great success is normally constructed of numerous well-crafted and interlaced components. So, it would be difficult indeed to duplicate them all in your business efforts or to specify the decisive one. But that's not the case with mistakes. A single mistake—whether caused by a lack of essential knowledge, an overblown belief in one's abilities, or a naïve set of economic expectations—can bring everything crumbling down. Therefore it makes sense to not only develop your own "inanities list," stocked with the business missteps and mishaps of others, but you should consult that list whenever important choices and decisions arise. Of course it goes without saying that listing the struts of business triumphs will be potentially helpful too, but any entry on the list won't have nearly the potential game-changing impact.

There is a second reason that supports the construction of your own inanities list. Even though we have been brainwashed to believe that positive information is always better than negative information, that's simply not true. In fact, after an extensive review of relevant research, respected scholar Roy Baumeister and his colleagues concluded that people "attend to, learn from, and use negative information far more than positive information."

But that's not all: Downside information is also more memorable and is typically given more weight in decision making. Accordingly, if you want to create an inventory of items that is likely to grab you and your team's attention, be easy to learn from, linger longer in memory, and offer instructive advice that spurs you to real action, you would be advised to construct a list that looks more like Charlie Munger's and less like the best practices you are most proud of.

There is a third benefit to listing and then learning from others' worst practices. Because your list will be comprised of the gaffes that someone else has made, it will be much easier to recognize them for the clunkers that they are. If they were your own mistakes, you would have to fight—often unsuccessfully—the inclination to convince yourself that they weren't mistakes at all, but instead simply instances of bad luck or unfortunate timing outside of your control. But the outward-directed character of others' prior lapses in judgment avoids that ego-defending bias and offers up a highly effective teaching tool for your own benefit. It's a benefit that can be extended to team members, too. That is, the astute leader can point to the mistakes of others rather than of teammates to steer their future behavior and sidestep the resentment that sometimes comes from direct criticism of one's colleagues.

By the way, the potential upsides of listing others' previous downsides aren't limited to the business environment.

Educators need not be shy in highlighting errors made by former students when constructing a "things to avoid" list for current students. A doctor, keen to ensure that a patient avoids situations in which a current medical condition could be exacerbated, would be advised to allude to a previous patient or two who made such a mistake and regretted it. A personal trainer could point a new client to prior mistakes made by others when using exercise equipment as a way of ensuring that they avoid the same errors and get the best out of their training regime.

Jim Collins is the impressively gifted author of best-selling business books such as *Good to Great* and *Built to Last* that describe what others have done right to achieve significant commercial success. He's convinced that access to this kind of information will help you achieve success as well. Charlie Munger is at least as renowned for his own intellectual gifts and financial savvy. Yet he recommends creating, and regularly consulting, a list populated not by instances of what others have done right but by instances of what they've done wrong.

Is there a way to reconcile these seemingly opposing recommendations from two great business minds? There may well be. It's noteworthy that one of Collins's more recent pieces of advice, contained in his book *How the Mighty Fall*, spotlights the major reasons that businesses fail—for example, denial of risk, unwarranted haste, and lack of intellectual discipline. We'd wager that vivid occurrences of each of those reasons exist on Charlie Munger's inanities list. It appears, then, that both men are saying something similar after all—*one small thing that leads to right moves in business is to have ready access to a catalog of others' wrong moves.* The first key step is to create one, refer to it frequently, and use it systematically when making important choices. It's a small thing that could make a big difference.

Of course failure to adopt this small BIG would be to ignore consistent research findings and sage advice regarding the value of documented errors…that in itself could be a mistake worthy of your list.

## CHAPTER 48

# How could a SMALL shift from error banishment to error management lead to BIG success?

In the last chapter, we covered what is known about ways you can benefit from the past mistakes of others. The topic of this chapter concerns what is known about ways you can benefit from your *own* past mistakes.

Lifespan researchers have concluded that a history of setbacks, losses, or hardships—if they are handled constructively—gives people not downbeat, damaged, tentative personalities but upbeat, healthy, confident ones. But does the same apply to your professional development, too? Put another way, could a shift in context so that your business takes steps to actively manage—rather than banish—mistakes and setbacks lead to big differences in its overall success and profitability?

Emerging evidence from something called Error Management Training (EMT) suggests that it well might. Of course the critical component of the process lies in the "if handled constructively" stipulation for success. When previous missteps are handled constructively, two major payoffs emerge. Not only will they act as good guides for future improvement, but they can even provide good opportunities for your future influence attempts, too.

Traditional training approaches are typically designed to guide trainees through a learning environment that is based

on examples of success and where the elimination of slipups
is emphasized and desirable. These conventional methods
seem reasonable because errors can disrupt workflow, be time-
consuming to fix, and frustrate the trainee as well as their trainer.
They might even erode the confidence of both in that trainee's
abilities. However when organizational scientists Nina Keith
and Michael Frese examined the results of 24 separate studies,
they found the Error Management model, despite running
wholly counter to the traditional error-avoidance approach to
training, to be far superior.

There are two necessary components to EMT. The first
involves urging trainees to actively undertake "to be learned"
tasks in order to encounter mistakes and therefore recognize
where and how they occur. The second component involves
instruction in how best to react, psychologically, once an error is
made. One especially important instruction concerns how the
trainer provides feedback to trainees. Small changes in the way
feedback is delivered— for example, by using phrases such as
"Errors are a natural part of the learning process;" "The more
errors you make, the more you learn;" and "Errors teach you
what you are still able to learn"—are crucial and can make a big
difference, because without them mistakes are more likely to
be experienced as defeats rather than as guideposts to success.
Given the importance of this orientation to successful corporate
cultures, it's no wonder that IDEO, one of the world's most
innovative companies, has a motto of "Fail often in order to
succeed sooner."

But what happens when the goal ceases to be about training
optimally for job responsibilities and instead becomes how to
execute those responsibilities optimally on the job? Under
those circumstances, the first component of Error Management Training—to look for chances to fumble the ball—is far
from a winning game plan when dealing with real customers,

coworkers, and superiors. However, the second component—thinking of and responding to missteps as learning opportunities—still provides a professional advantage. The advice here is, rather than playing the role of being an error hunter, position yourself in the role of an error opportunist. The error opportunist looks to cash in on any unintended stumble by learning from it in the recognition that both the individual and the organization can profit in the long run—profits that can, according to statistics cited by Professor Frese, turn out to be pretty handsome indeed. Compared to companies with a weak error management culture, *those with a strong error management culture are four times more likely to be among the most profitable companies in their industry.*

It turns out that managers who take the necessary steps to foster a working environment of error opportunism rather than error hunting can benefit in other ways, too. A while ago a colleague of ours, Brian Ahern, sent us an article from a sales magazine describing the shock that the COO of a global hotel chain got after reviewing the results of the very costly "Seamless Customer Experience" program his company had put into place. It wasn't the guests who had a seamless stay who reported the highest satisfaction ratings and future loyalty—rather, it was those who experienced a service stumble that was *immediately put right* by the hotel staff. There are several ways to understand why this occurs. For example, it may be that, after guests know that the organization can efficiently fix mistakes, they become more confident that the same will be true in any future dealings, leaving them with more favorable feelings toward the organization overall. We don't doubt this possibility, but we have a hunch that another factor is at work too. The remedy may well be perceived by guests as "special assistance," as something the hotel has gone out of its way to provide. By virtue of the rule for reciprocation, the hotel then becomes deserving of something special in return in the form of superior ratings and loyalty.

At a business conference, one of us overheard support for this reciprocity-based explanation when the general manager of the conference resort hotel related an incident that had occurred that very day. A guest had wanted to play tennis with her two young children, but the two child-size racquets the resort maintained were already in use. So, the general manager had a staffer drive immediately to a local sporting goods store, purchase another pair, and deliver them to his guest within 20 minutes of her request. Afterward, the mother stopped by the general manager's office and said, "I've just booked our entire extended family into this resort for the Fourth of July weekend because of what you did for me."

Isn't it interesting that had the resort stocked those additional two children's racquets from the outset—in order to ensure its guests a "seamless experience"—their availability would not have been viewed as a notable gift or service that warranted special gratitude and subsequent loyalty in return? In fact, the racquets may have hardly registered as a blip on Mom's resort-experience screen.

What's the implication for you? Is it a good idea to manufacture thin spots in the ice for clients or coworkers to fall through so you can be there to extricate them? Not at all. That would ultimately lead to the perception that dealing with you often requires some form of rescue. Much preferred is the simple recognition that people's expectations are perhaps too high and modern business is too complex to be rendered error-free; honest mistakes will occur. The key is to recognize that directing resources (attention, training systems, staff, budgets) toward the utopian goal of preventing all such glitches is likely to be less effective (and much more expensive) than directing resources to the goal of resolving our mistakes and problems quickly and to high levels of satisfaction.

By no means does all this imply that quality control is unimportant. But it's a fool's errand to chase performance perfection, because—besides the reality that everyone's fallibly human after all—"perfection" means so many different things to different people that it can't feasibly be arranged for ahead of time. Error correction, on the other hand, can be customized to the aggrieved person's view of what will constitute a satisfactory, and satisfying, outcome.

It seems that it is the unique customizability of the *reaction* to an error that provides it with the potential to be experienced as a personalized gift or service, placing the giver in a heightened position of influence, paradoxically, due to their gaffe.

In short, *problem-free* may not be as good in business as *problem-freed.*

## CHAPTER 49

# How could a SMALL change in timing make a BIG difference to your online reviews?

I n October 2013, the Fair Trade Commission of Taiwan fined the Samsung Corporation 10 million New Taiwan dollars (around US$350,000) for allegedly paying people to post reviews and comments on social media and websites attacking the products of Samsung's longtime rival HTC and at the same time praising its own.*

The case attracted much attention, primarily because there can be no doubting how reliant on online reviews people are when it comes to making decisions. For example, research conducted by the firm Penn Schoen Berland found that seven in ten Americans will consult online product reviews and consumer ratings before making a purchase. No surprise then that the Taiwanese Fair Trade Commission took prompt action against Samsung. As you'll recall from chapter 47, the scholar Roy Baumeister and his colleagues found that people "attend to, learn from, and use negative information far more than positive information."

This negativity bias, when considered in the context of an online environment, poses a considerable challenge for

---

*The practice of launching fictitious reviews as part of a grass roots campaign is known as "astro-turfing"—a reference to the fake grass commonly used in sports facilities in the 1980s.

individuals or organizations that rely on the reviews of previous customers to promote their business. If potential customers view positive reviews as less valuable than negative ones, what steps can a business take to increase the chances that positive reviews posted online will be seen as valuable—without resorting to underhanded or devious tactics such as the posting of fake negative reviews aimed at competitors?

It turns out there is one step in particular that we recommend. And as you probably guessed, it is a small and very effective one.

Marketing researchers Zoey Chen and Nicholas Lurie hypothesized that a positive online review would be seen as just as valuable as a negative one if the reviewer truthfully stated that the review was based on an experience that had happened that same day (for example, posting a review of a restaurant using statements such as "I just got back from this restaurant" or "my partner and I visited today").

One reason this might be the case is because it is pretty obvious that someone posting a negative review has likely had a genuinely poor experience. However, if they signal that their review is based on an experience they had that day, readers are more likely to assume that the positive review is a genuine reflection of the experience itself, rather than other explanations for the positive review, such as broadcasting to the world they have good taste in choosing where to dine, travel, etc.

To test their hypothesis, the researchers extracted over 65,000 reviews posted on Yelp.com about popular restaurants in five major US cities. In total they looked at reviews for almost 100 restaurants over the previous three years. For each review they measured the number of "useful" votes the review received from readers, the star rating that accompanied the review on a scale of 1 to 5 (5 stars indicated the most positive experience), and finally the presence of any words or phrases in the review

that indicated it had been written on the same day that the
restaurant was visited.

What they found was fascinating. When there were *no* cues
as to when the reviews had been written, the negative reviews
for that restaurant were voted as much more useful to readers
than the positive ones. However when it was clear that the
reviews had been written on the *same day* that the restaurant
had been visited, those who read the positive reviews voted
them as at least as useful as the negative ones.

In a separate online study, participants were randomly
assigned to one of four groups and asked to imagine they were
picking a restaurant for dinner. Each of the four groups was
then shown a review for "Joe's Restaurant." Two of the groups
were shown a review that was either positive or negative.
The other two groups were also shown either a positive or a
negative review, but this time the review mentioned that it had
been written on the day of the restaurant visit. Additionally, all
the groups were shown a neutral review for "Mike's Restaurant"
before being asked to select the restaurant they preferred, or to
choose neither.

Consistent with the finding from Yelp.com, when the review
was both positive and included the presence of a temporal cue,
it significantly increased the choice of Joe's Restaurant. In fact,
among participants who saw a timely and positive review, fully
100 percent chose to dine there.

If the timeliness of a positive review truly leads to that
review being viewed as more valuable, one small but important
change that marketers should make is to encourage consumers
to review products immediately after consumption and to
*explicitly* communicate that immediacy in their review. Many
restaurants will include a web address on the check inviting
diners to leave a review. This research suggests that changing
the usual "If you enjoyed your experience, please review us on

Yelp or TripAdvisor" to the more unusual "If you enjoyed your experience, please review us on Yelp or TripAdvisor and say you were here today!" could be a small difference that pays big dividends.

Web managers of online retailers should, after a transaction, include a link inviting customers to post a review of their experience. They should also include a pop-up reminding customers that their review will likely receive more "likes" if they highlight the fact that they made their purchase just minutes earlier.

People who review books online should recognize the potential benefits of including temporal references in their online posts, too. Doing so should not only benefit the authors but also the reviewers themselves, due to the likely increase in positive responses to their recommendations. In such situations all that remains is to decide which book you'll be waxing lyrical about.

Hey! We can think of one! ?

## CHAPTER 50

# What SMALL change can you make to an email that can make a BIG difference to how easy your business partners are to negotiate with?

Affectionately known as the Clown Prince of Denmark, Victor Borge, the much-loved Danish-American humorist, entertainer, and pianist, was reputed to have said that "laughter is the shortest distance between two people."

Laughter connects people, builds relationships, and, according to research conducted by a team of persuasion scientists, can even be a profitable business tool when it comes to negotiating with others online.

In our increasingly global economy, an estimated 850 million corporate email accounts now send and receive an average of 110 emails per day, and not just for routine messaging. Many businesses now use these exchanges as a primary means of working through quite complex interactions. Take negotiations for example. When negotiations occur between parties who are remote from each other, email becomes an attractive and efficient means of communication, allowing vendors to reach greater numbers of potential clients and customers to connect with a multitude of suppliers.

In many instances email exchanges can act as a useful and cost-effective filter prior to formal negotiations. For example, a potential purchaser may reach out by email to a short list of suppliers, with the parties exchanging messages before a decision is made to progress to phone calls, video conferencing, or perhaps Skype or FaceTime communication. Finally (and by this point it is by no means guaranteed) a face-to-face meeting might be agreed in order to conclude the negotiations.

So given their ubiquitous nature, how can you use emails to influence the development of the trust that is so important to successful business transactions?

In a wonderful series of studies, Terri Kurtzberg and her colleagues Charles E. Naquin and Liuba Belkin wanted to study the role that humor plays during the initial stages of a series of email exchanges in business and negotiation settings. The studies looked at whether the use of humor had any resulting impact on the levels of trust that were developed between negotiating parties, as well as any impact on the commercial outcomes gained by the parties concerned.

In one of their studies Kurtzberg and her colleagues arranged for teams of business professionals to negotiate a specific and reasonably complex contract via email. Half the study participants were paired up with their negotiation opponents and simply told to get down to business. The other half were instructed to first email their opponent a cartoon in which Scott Adams's Dilbert ruins a negotiation: first by trying to accept an offer before it's been made and then—also before any offer has been made—by alluding to an alternative and "better" offer from another party. To check that the cartoon was both effective at inducing laughter and also inoffensive, the researchers conducted a pre-test with a different group of businesspeople in advance. (It was found to be both.)

The researchers hypothesized that offering the cartoon before the negotiation began would create increased levels of trust between the negotiators, eventually leading to higher gains. And they were exactly right. The group who initiated the negotiation by sending the cartoon generated high levels of trust which, in turn, led to a 15 percent greater commercial outcome. That's a pretty impressive difference for such a small change.

So far, so good. But what about situations where the flexibility of the negotiations is limited? Many organizations, in an attempt to mitigate the variability of their negotiation outcomes, will set out pricing structures or limit the items on which negotiations can be conducted, such as credit terms and delivery schedules. In such situations, would opening the exchange with a humorous cartoon still influence outcomes?

When the researchers tested this, the negotiators who were sent the cartoon first were *more than twice* as likely to send a first offer that was within the boundaries of an acceptable bargaining arena compared to those that weren't sent the cartoon. In short, this single, simple, small change resulted in much more efficient negotiating and increased levels of trust between the parties.

The immediate implications seem obvious. In a time-constrained context it's easy to rattle off a curt and pithy email to others, if only in an attempt to cross another item off your burgeoning to-do list. But this study suggests that doing so, especially at the early stages of a negotiation, could turn out to be an expensive mistake.

Accordingly an investment of even just one extra minute to humanize your initial exchanges can be important. As the researchers suggest, "Having some sense of 'the other side' as a real person and not just an email address seems to help negotiators build trust and rapport, and thus create better agreements with each other." In fact, additional studies conducted by Kurtzberg and several other researchers found that volunteering personal information in the opening exchanges of an online negotiation in an attempt to uncover a connection with the "other side" not only reduced deadlocks in those subsequent negotiations but also increased commercial outcomes for both parties concerned.

Clearly we are not suggesting that in an attempt to increase the engagement and response rates of your email messages you divulge information so personal that it puts you at a potential risk (or simply scares the wits out of the recipient). But a snippet of information about your previous work experiences or perhaps an interest you have that is likely to be shared with the recipient of your email could be a small change that might make for a notable difference when relationship building online.

Note also that it may not be enough to simply send a funny cartoon. The specific cartoon employed in these studies was one chosen not only because of its ability to raise a chuckle. It was also entirely consistent with the task that the parties were about to undergo—namely, a negotiation. As a result, when employing laughter as an engagement strategy, consider not just the likelihood that your attempt will raise a smile, but to what extent your communication is aligned to the subject or matter you are about to discuss. And remember that sometimes it might be just as effective to discard the idea of an email completely and engage in a little friendly face-to-face chitchat or make a call instead.

In a competitive market where businesses are looking for any small changes they can make to increase their response rates and engagement without costing the earth, Victor Borge's point is a poignant one. When communicating with disparate groups, sometimes the closest point between two people is laughter—not just online but in face-to-face negotiations as well. For example, research conducted by Karen O'Quinn and Joel Aronoff found that negotiators who received a demand along with a joke ("Well, my final offer is $____, and I'll throw in my pet frog") conceded more financially than those who received the demand alone. But for those of you who are unwilling to part ways with your favorite amphibian just to close a deal, perhaps you could offer to throw in your favorite Dilbert cartoon instead.

## CHAPTER 51

# How might a SMALL touch lead to a BIG increase in value?

As the Greek legend goes, the god Dionysus offered King Midas a reward of his choosing for acting kindly toward Dionysus's friend. Midas requested that everything he touch turn to gold, a power that was immediately granted by Dionysus. Of course, we all know this is a fairy tale—objects can't simply turn into gold because they're touched.

Or can they?

Consumer researchers Joann Peck and Suzanne Shu believed that although physically touching a product might not exactly turn it into gold, it could very well increase its perceived value. Although this idea may not seem intuitively obvious— after all, think of how many retailers discourage touching of their products with "Please don't touch" or "Touch only with your eyes" signs—Peck and Shu hypothesized that touching something can create an emotional connection with it. The researchers noted they were in good company in holding this belief: Star Trek's Captain Jean-Luc Picard felt this way as well.

> **Captain Jean-Luc Picard:** It's a boyhood fantasy…I must have seen this ship hundreds of times in the Smithsonian but I was never able to touch it.

> **Lieutenant Commander Data:** Sir, does tactile contact alter your perception?
>
> **Captain Jean-Luc Picard:** Oh yes! For humans, touch can connect you to an object in a very personal way.

> (From *Star Trek: First Contact*)

In one experiment designed to test this idea, participants playing the role of potential buyers were shown two products—a coffee mug and a Slinky toy. In the study, half the potential buyers were explicitly instructed to touch and feel the products but the other half were explicitly told not to touch them. Afterward each potential buyer was asked how strongly they agreed with statements such as "I feel like this is my Slinky/Mug," "I feel a very high degree of personal ownership of the Slinky/Mug," and "I feel like I own this Slinky/Mug." They were also asked their opinion as to the value of both products.

The results clearly demonstrated that those participants who were able to touch the products reported a much higher positive emotional reaction to those products, and that tactile contact led to a greater sense of ownership. The combination of the higher positive emotions, coupled with the enhanced sense of ownership, increased those participants' perceived values of the mug and the Slinky—typically by a third more than those who explicitly were told not to touch them. That's a pretty significant upward shift for a small change that requires nothing other than to provide an opportunity for someone to touch what is on offer. Interestingly, the researchers also found a similar pattern of results with sellers as well—when selling items they had been given earlier, the sellers demanded higher prices for items they had touched than those they hadn't.

This research is important for several reasons. As a consumer, it is important to understand and recognize the factors that affect our judgments and decisions. When a retailer asks us to touch or hold an item in our hands, its perceived value will automatically increase after doing so.

Similarly, a seller who arranges for potential buyers to feel more of a connection to the goods being sold by giving them the item to touch could be making a small change that leads to a big difference. For example, the packing for many of Paper Mate's pens has a section of the package cut out, which allows prospective consumers to touch the pen; this not only enables potential customers to see how the pen feels, but also enhances the value of the product.

Supermarkets and food stores might also benefit from the value-enhancing qualities of touch. Some stores, for entirely understandable reasons related to good food hygiene, might frown on consumers who handle loose and unpackaged products such as fruits, vegetables, and bakery goods. However, in the knowledge that they will likely have to discard a certain amount of spoiled stock anyway, perhaps having "touching sections" that actively encourage customers to handle goods might be a potentially profitable thing to do.

In addition to the peddling of pens, peaches, and pumpernickel, the subtle but powerful persuasiveness of touch might enhance the value of your printed materials too. When submitting that report to a manager or tendering your proposal to a potential client, try to print off the document and hand it to them rather than send it electronically. Lecturers, workshop leaders, and corporate trainers, who leave course materials on tables might instead be advised to hand materials directly to their students and delegates as they enter the room. To increase the perceived value of gifts and goodies provided by sponsors and given out at conferences and conventions, meeting and event managers might arrange for a selected item to be taken from the bag and personally handed over, thereby ensuring that not only is its value potentially enhanced but also that the chances of that item languishing in the bottom of a carry bag are eliminated.

But what about those situations where the ability to touch a product *before* purchasing it is limited? With increasing numbers of people turning to online environments to make their purchases, there are likely to be lots of potential customers who will never have the opportunity to touch your offerings before they get delivered to their door. Does this mean that you'll have to give up on the idea of providing touch until Google invents a *Star Trek*–like transporter that delivers a product to your customer over the web so consumers can touch it before purchase?

Actually, no.

In their studies, Peck and Shu found that when a product was unavailable to touch, a different small BIG procedure could be effective: Simply asking a customer *to imagine* touching the product was enough to increase perceived ownership and, consequently, its value.

However, it is also important to be aware of a crucial exception to this research. According to Peck and Shu, asking consumers to touch products is *only* beneficial if the products are either neutral or pleasant to touch.

Porcupine salesmen beware!

## CHAPTER 52

# Saving the best 'til last. What SMALL BIG can make all the difference?

First impressions count. But as any pop star or film director will tell you, what happens at the end is important, too. And focusing attention on, or making subtle changes to, the way an interaction ends, a business transaction is completed, or even what you do on the last day of your vacation can have an incredible influence on outcomes as diverse as your customer satisfaction scores, whether you get repeat business and attract client loyalty, or even how much you enjoy your next vacation.

Imagine for a few moments that you have just visited your physician's office for a routine but rather uncomfortable medical procedure and, on leaving the examination room, you are asked how painful it was and how much you are looking forward to your next examination. By way of contrast, now imagine this much more pleasant scenario. You have just returned from your vacation, and you are asked how much you enjoyed it and how much you are looking forward to your next one.

If you are like most people in various studies who have been asked these questions, then your responses will most likely be influenced by two things: The peak moment of intensity you felt during the experience—pain in the case of the medical checkup and (hopefully) pleasure in the case of your vacation—and the final moments of the experience. Those who first studied this phenomenon referred to it as the *peak-end effect*.

Rather surprisingly, your feelings at any other time of the experience matter a lot less than you might think. Furthermore your overall evaluation of the experience will most likely also suffer from something called *duration neglect*, meaning that you will tend to pay less attention to how long an experience lasted and, on some occasions, will disregard its duration entirely.

One classic study in particular, conducted by Nobel Prize–winner Daniel Kahneman and medical doctor Donald Redelmeier, brilliantly demonstrated how patients who had undergone a painful medical procedure (a colonoscopy) were much more likely to recall *afterward* how much pain they experienced (a) at the peak moment of discomfort and (b) at the end of the examination.

Peak-end effects are the reason why pop stars tend to play their most popular songs at the end of the concert. They also explain why the waiter who was rude at the end of your meal can totally spoil your memory of an otherwise lovely experience. And remember that incredibly boring meeting you were in last week—the one that you thought would never end? On reflection it doesn't seem so long now does it? That's duration neglect in action.

Given that our memories of the experiences we encounter are etched into our minds with extremity and recency but not necessarily duration, they can be a less-than-perfect guide when we decide how we feel about what we have experienced. But regardless of how imperfect a guide memories may be, they can still have an enormous influence over our future decisions. As a result, if you want to foster future collaboration with others, encourage greater customer loyalty, or simply get better feedback, while the advice would be to focus on the whole experience, you would be especially advised to make small changes that amplify the high points of the experience (or minimize the low points) and to enrich the very last thing that happens.

Lots of people like chocolate and regard Swiss chocolate as the very best in the world, so on a recent flight with the country's national airline, one of us was delighted to be given a Swiss chocolate on boarding the flight. One wonders if the impact of this small, yet smart, gesture could be amplified further by giving travelers the chocolate as they leave, rather than only as they board, the airplane.

Similarly we have noticed that some hotels provide welcome gifts to their guests such as stationery items, branded bath products, and, on one occasion, a high-quality bottle opener. These items will often come accompanied with a handwritten note from the duty manager expressing the desire that the guests enjoy their stay. A small BIG shift that hotel managers might ponder is whether they could attain the best of both worlds by providing the personalized note as guests check in and the gift when they check out.

Web designers, too, could benefit from small BIGs aligned to the peak-end effect by arranging for a nice image or thank-you note to pop up as people log off a website. Or, in the case of an online purchase, arrange for a surprise piece of content or a voucher for the future to be made available. Nurses could give kids (and we suspect some adults, too) a candy or a sticker for being brave at vaccination time. Of course this already happens in many clinics and health centers although probably not with this effect in mind.

Focusing on the small BIGs that can be made at the end of interactions and experiences needn't just be limited to those more obvious transactions that occur, such as in the travel and hospitality industries. There are notable public sector applications, too. For example, a hospital patient's memory of an otherwise highly satisfactory (and expensive) medical procedure could very easily be overshadowed if their very last experience before leaving the hospital is to be kept waiting for hours in a dreary room or corridor for transport home. Given the increasing importance that NHS hospitals place on patient satisfaction rates one way they could ensure that memories of a stay are largely positive would be to send patients home in a nice taxi. Of course where a hospital wishes an individual's memory of an experience to be less positive, for example in the case of a patient attending an A&E when it would have been more appropriate for them to visit a local pharmacy or a walk-in centre they might consider making the final moments of their visit less pleasant.

More controversially, a case could be made that inmates incarcerated in prisons might be less likely to reoffend if the final days before their release are the most painful of their sentence and not, as is more usually the case, the easiest.

The finding that people's memories of previous experiences will often suffer from duration neglect might prompt a small change to a common strategy employed by salespeople and marketers to persuade customers to switch from one product to an alternative. When addressing the specific pain points that a potential customer may experience with an existing product, rather than focusing on the wasted time caused by such problems, it would be better for marketers and sales professionals to focus on the intensity of the pain the customer experiences when such problems occur.

Understanding the influence that these peak-end effects have when it comes to evaluating our own experiences can also prompt small changes that lead to big effects. If you want to have fabulous memories of your next vacation, rather than spreading your budget thinly by booking lots of small excursions and day trips, you'd be much better off spending a bigger chunk of your budget on two amazing experiences, including one at the end. And rather than using those free miles to get a nicer seat on the way out, you'll likely be much better off if you travel *back* home in style instead.

Business authors too might increase the odds of positive reader reviews on Amazon and recommendations to friends and colleagues by paying special attention to the end of their book to ensure that their readers' memories are positive ones. To this end, while we may have reached the last of our 52 small BIG chapters, we have included a bonus chapter that, when coupled with your favorite chapter, provides you with a peak-end positive experience of your own.

# The SMALL BIG: Bonus chapter

O ur goal in this book has been to provide a collection of small BIGs that you can add to your persuasion toolkit. Small changes, informed by recent persuasion science that anyone—from businesspeople to healthcare professionals, politicians to parents—can employ to make a big difference when persuading and communicating with others.

Although the 52 small BIGs we have presented differ from each other in some way, such as the psychological mechanism that drives them or the contexts or situations where they can be most successfully deployed, they share an important similarity. When used responsibly and in the right context, each can afford the communicator a significant advantage when attempting to influence others.

But the idea that a single small BIG, used ethically and in the appropriate context, can make a big difference prompts another question: To what extent can multiple small BIGs, used either in sequence or in combination, lead to even greater results? For example, is it the case that shoehorning as many individual small BIG strategies into your influence attempts will make your persuasion efforts even more productive?

The answer is clearly no. Just as you would never use every single tool in your toolkit to accomplish a single fix-it job around the house, trying to use too many tools of persuasion at once could actually make it more difficult to achieve the outcome you are hoping for. While there is emerging evidence that some influence strategies can work well in combination there is also evidence that in certain contexts, not only will one cancel out another, but will actually lead to a worse result than if no persuasion strategy was employed at all.

Here are some examples that illustrate each of these scenarios.

Cast your mind back to chapter 8, where we described our research showing how health center managers could reduce the number of patients who failed to show up for their appointments simply by asking patients to make a verbal commitment by repeating back their appointment time before hanging up the phone. Remember also how, in a second study, asking patients to write down appointment details on a reminder card themselves, rather than reception staff doing it, produced an even bigger effect, reducing no-shows by 18 percent. We tested another strategy, too. For a period of several months we replaced the signs in health center waiting rooms that highlighted the large number of people who had previously failed to attend appointments with signs that communicated the much larger social proof of the situation—the number of people who did turn up. When these three small BIG strategies were used in combination we measured a 31.4 percent reduction in subsequent nonattendance. To demonstrate that it was the combination of these small changes making this big difference and not some other, unrelated factor, we stopped the interventions and no-shows rose dramatically. As soon as we reengaged the combination of the three small changes, no-shows fell again by an average of 30 percent and in doing so demonstrated how a combination of several small changes can lead to even bigger differences.

So far, the case for combining persuasion strategies is looking good. However, before we get carried away, let's note that this is not always the case. Take, for example, a wonderful series of studies conducted by behavioral scientists Paul Dolan and Robert Metcalfe. In their experiments they found that informing households about how they were consuming more energy than their neighbors was a small change that led to a big difference. Energy consumption in those households declined by an average of 6 percent in subsequent months.

They also found that offering householders a £100 ($150) reward if they reduced their energy consumption was pretty effective, too. Consumption dropped by a similar amount as for those who received the information that pointed to their being out of step with their neighbors.

But what happens when you combine the social norm approach with the incentive approach? Fortunately, the researchers considered this question and carried out an experiment in which another group of householders was told how their consumption compared to their neighbors' and at the same time was offered £100 if they reduced it. What happened?

The strategy had absolutely no effect on consumption whatsoever!

At first glance, this makes no apparent sense. In mathematics if you add one and one you get two. In this study adding one and one didn't even result in a bit more than one. It resulted in zero! Nothing. Nil points. It was as if one successful persuasion strategy cancelled out an equally successful strategy to such an extent that it would have been better to save on the postage and do nothing.

So what is going on? Why is it that certain combinations of persuasion strategies can work well together and enhance the overall result and others do not?

Here are three possible explanations.

The first concerns the incompatibility of underlying motivations that can be activated by a multifaceted message. For example, when being urged to conserve energy, the motivation to do so for personal gain (the £100 offered by the researchers) may have felt incompatible with the motivation to make a sacrifice for the common good (as validated by their neighbors). Consequently, these two strong but countervailing motivations may have cancelled each other out.

Therefore, when constructing an influence attempt that includes a combination of persuasive approaches, it is important to ensure that the approaches complement one another by activating compatible human motivations.

The second reason why combining multiple approaches to persuasion sometimes fails is that the more persuasion tools you use in a single attempt to influence another person, the less likely that person will be to engage with you (or your communication) in the first place. For example, if you are trying to persuade your boss to let you leave work early for the day, she is far more likely to immediately read and respond to a one-line, one-influence-technique email than an email containing six paragraphs full of dozens of techniques. This may be simply because she doesn't feel she has the time to thoroughly read the longer email. She may put off reading the email until it's too late, or may even forget about it entirely as her inbox fills up with other urgent (and presumably shorter and snappier) requests. Similarly, home residents may be more likely to disengage from, or "put aside for later" (never to be looked at again in actuality), home energy reports—or any direct marketing materials for that matter—that contain many tactics embedded in a large amount of written material.

A third reason why certain influence strategies will work in combination and others may fail relates to the obviousness of the influence attempt. Sometimes when a number of small changes are combined, they don't remain subtle but merge into a larger, much more explicit persuasion attempt, which can heighten resistance.

To give an example, in one study conducted by Daniel Feiler, Leigh Tost, and Adam Grant, 8,000 alumni of a large public university were sent an email asking if they would be willing to donate to the university. For some recipients the request was accompanied by a message pointing out the "egoistic" benefits of giving: "Previous alumni report that giving makes them feel good." Other recipients received the request accompanied by an altruistic reason: "Giving is your chance to make a difference to the lives of students, faculty, and staff." Finally another group received a request to donate highlighting both the egoistic reasons and the altruistic reasons for giving. Those who received both reasons were less than half as likely to donate as those given either one alone.

In another study by the same researchers, participants received a request to donate to the Make-A-Wish Foundation that had either two egoistic reasons to give, two altruistic reasons, or all four reasons combined. Again, giving intentions were much lower in the group that was provided with four reasons to donate. Post-study surveys revealed a simple reason why: People could see the message for what it was—an attempt to persuade them. It seems that when crafting a persuasive communication there comes a point when adding additional arguments and justifications acts to heighten resistance, which, in turn, greatly reduces the communication's impact.

So what is the optimal number of claims that should be used to produce the most positive impression?

To answer this important question, consider a study conducted by behavioral scientists Suzanne Shu and Kurt Carlson. In Shu and Carlson's study, participants were assigned to one of six groups and were asked to read descriptions of five different target objects—a breakfast cereal, a restaurant, a shampoo, an ice cream store, and a politician. As an example, the shampoo advertisement was introduced as follows:

Imagine that you are reading one of your favorite magazines and an ad for a new brand of shampoo catches your attention. You decide to read the ad carefully to see if it is worth switching to this new product. The ad says that this new shampoo does the following: <BLANK SPACE>

The blank space was then filled with one, two, three, four, five, or six positive claims about the shampoo. For example, participants who were shown all six claims read "Makes hair cleaner, stronger, healthier, softer, shinier, and fuller."

In the political advertisement participants who were shown all six claims read that the candidate was "honest, had integrity, experience, intelligence, interpersonal skills, and a desire to serve."

After the participants saw the ads, the researchers measured their attitudes toward each target product or person along with the positive or negative level of their impressions. The researchers also measured the participants' levels of skepticism in an attempt to locate the point at which people started to think that the claims in the ads were not there to inform them but to push them to choose a particular product.

The results clearly demonstrated that those who had read *three* claims rated all the subjects of the ads (regardless of whether they were breakfast cereals, politicians, etc.) significantly more positively than participants who had read the ads with one, two, four, five, or six claims. It appears that adding additional positive claims to a persuasive appeal increased its effectiveness up until the third claim was encountered. But after that, further persuasion attempts increased skepticism, which in turn heightened resistance to the overall persuasion appeal.

So it seems that, in this case at least, the answer to the question of what is the optimal number of claims that should be used to produce the most positive impression is three.

Or, as Shu and Carlson so succinctly concluded, "Three charms but four alarms."

These studies show that even as you use and combine these strategies in completely ethical ways, utilizing a large number of persuasive claims or tactics can make your influence target *think* that you may be acting less ethically than you truly are.

When it comes to influencing the way others think, feel, and act, small changes can make a big difference for one fundamental reason. They *are* small. They fly under the radar. They rarely raise suspicion or attention. Instead, they go quietly about their business shaping our decisions and influencing our behaviors in largely automatic and unconscious ways. In a world in which bigger is often equated with better, we're pleased not only that we've provided you with a whole toolkit full of ethical tools of influence, but that the tools themselves are so seemingly diminutive that they will hardly go noticed. And in that sense, when it comes to influence, small is most certainly the new BIG.

\* \* \*

To keep up to date with the latest insights from persuasion science and receive our free *Inside Influence Report* each month, visit: www.influenceatwork.co.uk

Follow Steve Martin on Twitter @scienceofyes

# Acknowledgments

As the saying goes, "It takes a village to raise a child." We think the same is true when it comes to raising a book. Accordingly there are many people who deserve our acknowledgment and gratitude.

As a team of authors who study both the science and practice of influence and persuasion we feel incredibly lucky to live in a village populated with so many dedicated and smart researchers who work tirelessly to advance the knowledge of the persuasion process and the lessons it can teach us. We would like to thank every one of these researchers, especially those whose work and insights we have drawn from in this book.

Additionally we would like to extend our thanks to Keith Anderson, Suraj Bassi, Rupert Dunbar-Rees, Paul Dolan, Bernie Goldstein, and James Nicholls, all of whom have influenced the work here.

While we were writing we were fortunate to have access to a group of folks willing to read early drafts of the chapters and suggest ideas for practically applying the insights contained within them. Thanks are due to Rob Blackie, Natalie Britt, Sean Buckland, Eilidh Connolly, Emma Rose Hurst, Benjamin Kaube, Gregor McPherson, Steve Mound, John Vincent, and James West.

We also wish to thank everyone in the US and UK offices of INFLUENCE AT WORK including Eily VanderMeer and Sarah Tobitt as well as everyone at our publishers, Business Plus/Grand Central Publishing in New York and Profile Books in London. Special thanks are due to our editors Rick Wolff, Mitch Hoffman, Daniel Crewe, and Penny Daniel whose support, encouragement, and insights have been invaluable to us. We would also like to extend thanks to Andrew Franklin, Clare Grist Taylor, and Flora Willis as well as to Ruth Killick Publicity, Turnbull Ripley and Tinopolis Interactive.

Three people in particular deserve to be singled out for special thanks. Danica Giles worked tirelessly as our researcher, checking and rechecking facts. Thank you for your support and help, Danica. You have been a Star!

From the outset our agent, Jim Levine at Levine Greenberg Rostan, has been a joy to work with. Jim, you and your team are the epitome of what a partnership is all about. Thank you so much.

And to Bobette Gorden, whose insight, boundless energy, and drive make her the unsung hero of this book.

Finally we would like to thank our loved ones and families for their support and love.

# Notes

## Introduction

The no-shows in health centers study can be found in: Martin, S. J., Bassi, S., & Dunbar-Rees, R. (2012). Commitments, norms and custard creams—a social influence approach to reducing did not attends (DNAs). *Journal of the Royal Society of Medicine* 105(3), 101–104. doi:10.1258/jrsm.2011.110250

The full reference for Robert Cialdini's book is: Cialdini, R. B. (2009). *Influence: Science and Practice* (5th ed.). Boston: Allyn & Bacon.

The full reference for the book *Yes!* is: Goldstein, N. J., Martin, S. J., & Cialdini, R. B. (2007). *Yes! 50 Secrets from the Science of Persuasion*. London: Profile Books.

## 1. What small BIG can persuade people to pay their taxes on time?

For more details on the tax letter study, see: Martin, S. J. (2012). 98% of HBR readers love this article. *Harvard Business Review* 90, 23–25.

For a review of compliance and conformity research in light of the three fundamental human motivations described, see: Cialdini, R. B., Goldstein, N. J. (2004). Social influence: Compliance and conformity. *Annual Review of Psychology* 55, 591–621. doi:10.1146/annurev.psych.55.090902.142015

The household energy conservation study can be found in: Schultz, P. W., Nolan, J. M., Cialdini, R. B., Goldstein, N. J., & Griskevicius, V. (2007). The constructive, destructive, and reconstructive power of social norms. *Psychological Science* 18(5), 429–434. doi:10.1111/j.1467–9280.2007.01917.x

The account of commuters giving money to a musician can be found in: Cialdini, R. B. (2007). Descriptive social norms as underappreciated sources of social control. *Psychometrika* 72(2), 263–268.

Following on from our initial HMRC work, a comprehensive series of studies has been conducted by HMRC and the UK Government. For more, see Hallsworth, M., List, J. A., Metcalfe, R. D., & Vlaev, I. (2014). The behavioralist as tax collector: Using natural field experiments to enhance tax compliance. *National Bureau of Economic Research* working paper no. 20007.

## 2. What small BIG can persuade people to go against the crowd?

Asch's original conformity studies can be found in: Asch, S. E. (1951). Effects of group pressure upon the modification and distortion of judgments. *Groups, Leadership, and Men*, 222–236.

The research on Mexican waves can be found in: Farkas, I., Helbing, D., & Vicsek, T. (2002). Mexican waves in an excitable medium. *Nature* 419(6903), 131–132. doi:10.1038/419131a

The brain-imaging studies on conformity can be found in: Berns, G. S., Chappelow, J., Zink, C. F., Pagnoni, G., Martin-Skurski, M. E., & Richards, J. (2005). Neurobiological correlates of social conformity and independence during mental rotation. *Biological Psychiatry* 58(3), 245–253.

For an in-depth review of the digital, technology, and analytics operations of President Barack Obama's reelection campaign, visit Inside the Cave at: http://enga.ge/projects/inside-the-cave/.

For a more detailed history of persuasion strategies applied to political campaigns, see Issenberg, S. (2012). *The Victory Lab: The Secret Science of Winning Campaigns*. New York: Crown Books. It is well worth a read.

The study investigating people's divergence from *out*-group choices can be found in: Berger, J., & Heath, C. (2008). Who drives divergence? Identity signaling, outgroup dissimilarity, and the abandonment of cultural tastes. *Journal of Personality and Social Psychology* 95(3), 593.

## 3. What small change to the way you frame a message can lead to BIG differences in outcome?

The "sneezy" study can be found in: Blanton, H., Stuart, A. E., & Van den Eijnden, R. J. J. M. (2001). An introduction to deviance-regulation theory: The effect of behavioral norms on message framing. *Personality and Social Psychology Bulletin* 27(7), 848–858. doi:10.1177/0146167201277007

The healthy practices study can be found in: Blanton, H., Van den Eijnden, R. J. J. M., Buunk, B. P., Gibbons, F. X., Gerrard, M., & Bakker, A. (2001). Accentuate the negative: Social images in the prediction and promotion of condom use. *Journal of Applied Social Psychology* 31(2), 274–295. doi:10.1111/j.1559–1816.2001. tb00197.x

## 4. What small BIG can help to right a wrong?

For more on James Wilson's and George Kelling's work on the broken-window theory, see: Wilson, J., & Kelling, G. (1982). Broken windows. *Atlantic Monthly* 249(3), 29–38.

The bicycle littering study, the fence study, and the mailbox study can all be found in: Keizer, K., Lindenberg, S., & Steg, L. (2008). The spreading of disorder. *Science* 322(5908), 1681–1685. doi:10.1126/science.1161405

The research on the encouragement of desirable behaviors can be found in: Keizer, K., Lindenberg, S., & Steg, L. (2013). The importance of demonstratively restoring order. *PLOS ONE* 8(6). e65137. doi:10.1371/journal.pone.0065137

The littering reduction study can be found in: Cialdini, R. B., Reno, R. R., & Kallgren, C. A. (1990). A focus theory of normative conduct: recycling the concept of norms to reduce littering in public places. *Journal of Personality and Social Psychology* 58(6), 1015.

## 5. How could a small change in name make a BIG difference to your game?

For the hurricane donation study, see: Chandler, J., Griffin, T. M., & Sorensen, N. (2008). In the "I" of the storm: Shared initials increase disaster donations. *Judgement and Decision Making* 3(5), 404–410.

The full reference for *Drunk Tank Pink* is: Alter, A. L. (2013). *Drunk Tank Pink: And Other Unexpected Forces that Shape How We Think, Feel, and Behave.* New York: Penguin.

For more on the Cocktail Party Phenomenon, see: Conway, A. R. A., Cowan, N., & Bunting, M. F. (2001). The cocktail party phenomenon revisited: The importance of working memory capacity. *Psychonomic Bulletin & Review* 8(2), 331–335.

The favorite letters study can be found in: Nuttin, J. (1985). Narcissism beyond Gestalt and awareness: The name letter effect. *European Journal of Social Psychology* 15, 353–361.

The finding that including a recipient's first name in SMS text messages can reduce subsequent no-shows is currently unpublished and part of a broader Demand and Capacity experiment conducted with a team of British physicians and the management consulting firm BDO. http://www.bdo.co.uk/

For the study that examined the effect of sending a text message requesting payment of a fine that included the offender's first name, see: Behavioural Insights Team (2012). *Applying Behavioural Insights to Reduce Fraud, Error and Debt.* London: Cabinet Office.

## 6. What small steps can lead to BIG leaps when building relationships, partnerships, and teamwork?

The soccer fans study can be found in: Levine, M., Prosser, A., & Evans, D. (2005). Identity and emergency intervention: How social group membership and inclusiveness of group boundaries shape helping behavior. *Personality and Social Psychology Bulletin* 31(4), 443–453.

The full reference for *Give and Take* is: Grant, A. (2013). *Give and Take—A Revolutionary Approach to Success*. New York: Viking.

## 7. What small BIG can help you to become wiser with experience?

You can find the preference predictions study in: Scheibehenne, B., Mata, J., & Todd, P. M. (2011). Older but not wiser—Predicting a partner's preferences gets worse with age. *Journal of Consumer Psychology* 21(2), 184–191. doi:10.1016/j.jcps.2010.08.001

## 8. What small BIGs can persuade people to keep their appointments with you?

The data source of the overall cost to the UK health department caused by no-shows is: *BBC News*. (2009, August). "No shows" cost the NHS millions. http://news.bbc.co.uk/1/hi/health/8195255.stm

The beach theft study can be found in: Moriarty, T. (1975). Crime, commitment, and the responsive bystander: Two field experiments. *Journal of Personality and Social Psychology* 31(2), 370–376. doi:10.1037/h0076288

The studies examining reduction of no-shows can be found in: Martin, S. J., Bassi, S., & Dunbar-Rees, R. (2012). Commitments, norms and custard creams—a social influence approach to reducing did not attends (DNAs). *Journal of the Royal Society of Medicine* 105(3), 101–104. doi:10.1258/jrsm.2011.110250

### 9. What small BIG can help your influence attempts to win over and over?

For the full reference for our book *Yes!*, see research notes to the Introduction.

For the hotel towel study, see: Goldstein, N. J., Cialdini, R. B., & Griskevicius, V. (2008). A room with a viewpoint: Using social norms to motivate environmental conservation in hotels. *Journal of Consumer Research* 35(3), 472–482. doi:10.1086/586910

The study investigating commitment related to environmental protection in hotels can be found in: Baca-Motes, K., Brown, A., Gneezy, A., Keenan, E. A., & Nelson, L. D. (2013). Commitment and behavior change: Evidence from the field. *Journal of Consumer Research* 39(5), 1070–1084. doi:10.1086/667226

### 10. What small BIG can ensure your influence attempts don't backfire?

The licensing effect studies can be found in: Catlin, J. R., & Wang, Y. (2013). Recycling gone bad: When the option to recycle increases resource consumption. *Journal of Consumer Psychology* 23(1), 122–127. doi:10.1016/j.jcps.2012.04.001

### 11. What small BIG should you add to your recipe for employee productivity?

For the task significance study, see: Grant, A. M. (2008). The significance of task significance: Job performance effects, relational mechanisms, and boundary conditions. *The Journal of Applied Psychology* 93(1), 108–124. doi:10.1037/0021-9010.93.1.108

## 12. What small BIG should you look to avoid when it comes to successfully making decisions?

The vicarious entrapment studies can be found in: Gunia, B. C., Sivanathan, N., & Galinsky, A. D. (2009). Vicarious entrapment: Your sunk costs, my escalation of commitment. *Journal of Experimental Social Psychology* 45(6), 1238–1244. doi:10.1016/j.jesp.2009.07.004

The study that demonstrates how assigning others to judge can minimize self-enhancement bias can be found in: Pfeffer, J., Cialdini, R. B., Hanna, B., & Knopoff, K. (1998). Faith in supervision and self-enhancement bias. Two psychological reasons why managers don't empower workers. *Basic and Applied Social Psychology* 20, 313–321.

## 13. What small BIG is the key to planning persuasion?

For the voting study, see: Nickerson, D. W., & Rogers, T. (2010). Do you have a voting plan?: Implementation intentions, voter turnout, and organic plan making. *Psychological Science* 21(2), 194–199. doi:10.1177/0956797609359326

The Behavioural Insight Team job center study will be the subject of a future published report. The data can be accessed at http://blogs.cabinetoffice. gov.uk/behavioural-insights-team/2012/12/14/ new-bit-trial-results-helping-people-back-into-work/.

For the flu vaccination study, see: Milkman, K. L., Beshears, J., Choi, J. J., Laibson D., & Madrian, B. C. (2011). Using implementation intentions prompts to enhance influenza vaccination rates. *Proceedings of the National Academy of Sciences* 108, 10415–10420.

## 14. What small BIG can lock people into your persuasion attempts?

The research investigating how people think about events that occur in the future can be found in: Trope, Y., & Liberman, N. (2003). Temporal construal. *Psychological Review* 110(3), 403.

A broader discussion of how people think and feel about the future can be found in the excellent Wilson, T. D., & Gilbert, D. T. (2003). Affective forecasting. *Advances in Experimental Social Psychology* 35, 345–411.

For the "future lock-in" commitment strategy study, see: Rogers, T., & Bazerman, M. H. (2008). Future lock-in: Future implementation increases selection of "should" choices. *Organizational Behavior and Human Decision Processes* 106(1), 1–20. doi:10.1016/j.obhdp.2007.08.001

You can read more about the "Save More Tomorrow" program in: Thaler, R., & Benartzi, S. (2004). Save more tomorrow™: Using behavioral economics to increase employee saving. *Journal of Political Economy* 112(1), S164–S187.

## 15. What small BIG do you owe it to yourself to act on?

The savings for retirement study can be found in: Bryan, C. J., & Hershfield, H. E. (2012). You owe it to yourself: Boosting retirement saving with a responsibility-based appeal. *Journal of Experimental Psychology: General* 141(3), 429.

The age-progression studies can be found in: Hershfield, H. E., Goldstein, D. G., Sharpe, W. F., Fox, J., Yeykelis, L., Carstensen, L. L., & Bailenson, J. N. (2011). Increasing saving behavior through age-progressed renderings of the future self. *Journal of Marketing Research* 48(SPL), S23–S37.

The impact of reminding people that although they may change their core identity remains the same can be found in: Bartels, D. M., & Urminsky, O. (2011). On inter-temporal selfishness: How the perceived instability of identity underlies impatient consumption. *Journal of Consumer Research* 38(1), 182–198.

## 16. What small BIG can reconnect people to their goals?

The high-low versus specific goal experiments can be found in: Scott, M. L., & Nowlis, S. M. (2013). The effect of goal specificity on consumer goal reengagement. *Journal of Consumer Research* 40(3), 444–459.

More on the factors that persuade people to pursue goals can be found in: Oettingen, G., Bulgarella, C., Henderson, M., & Gollwitzer, P. M. (2004), The self-regulation of goal pursuit. In R. A. Wright, J. Greenberg, and S. S. Brehm (Eds). *Motivational Analyses of Social Behavior: Building on Jack Brehm's Contributions to Psychology*. Mahwah, NJ: Erlbaum, 225–244.

## 17. What small BIGs can be used to make defaults more effective?

For the research on Enhanced Active Choice, see: Keller, P., Harlam, B., Loewenstein, G., & Volpp, K. G. (2011). Enhanced active choice: A new method to motivate behavior change. *Journal of Consumer Psychology* 21, 376–383.

## 18. What small BIG can reduce people's tendency to procrastinate? (And yours too!)

For the gift certificate studies, see: Shu, S., & Gneezy, A. (2010). Procrastination of enjoyable experiences. *Journal of Marketing Research* 47(5), 933–944.

The email invitations research can be found in: Porter, S. R., & Whitcomb, M. E. (2003). The impact of contact type on web survey response rates. *Public Opinion Quarterly* 67, 579–588.

## 19. What small BIG can keep your customers hooked?

The waiting-in-line research can be found in: Janakiraman, N., Meyer, R. J., & Hoch, S. J. (2011). The psychology of decisions to abandon waits for service. *Journal of Marketing Research* 48(6), 970–984.

## 20. What is the small BIG that could turn your potential into reality?

The potential versus achievement studies can be found in: Tormala, Z. L., Jia, J. S., & Norton, M. I. (2012). The preference for potential. *Journal of Personality and Social Psychology* 103(4), 567–583. doi:10.1037/a0029227

## 21. What small BIG could help you lead more productive meetings?

Titus and Stasser's research on group decision making can be found in: Stasser, G., & Titus, W. (1985). Pooling of unshared information in group decision making: Biased information sampling during discussion. *Journal of Personality and Social Psychology* 48(6), 1467–1478. doi:10.1037//0022–3514.48.6.1467

For the medical cases study, see: Larson, J. R., Christensen, C., Franz, T. M., & Abbott, S. (1998). Diagnosing groups: The pooling, management, and impact of shared and unshared case information in team-based medical decision making. *Journal of Personality and Social Psychology* 75(1), 93–108.

The full reference for *The Checklist Manifesto* is: Gawande, A. (2009). *The Checklist Manifesto: How to Get Things Right*. New York: Metropolitan Books.

The seating arrangements research can be found in: Zhu, R., & Argo, J. J. (2013). Exploring the impact of various shaped seating arrangements on persuasion. *Journal of Consumer Research* 40(2), 336–349. doi:10.1086/670392

## 22. What small BIG could ensure you are dressed for success?

For more on the powerful sway of the well-attired, see: Bickman, L. (1974). The social power of a uniform. *Journal of Applied Social Psychology* 4(1), 47–61.

The stethoscope research can be found in: Castledine, G. (1996). Nursing image: It is how you use your stethoscope that counts! *British Journal of Nursing* 5(14), 882.

For the jaywalker study, see: Lefkowitz, M., Blake, R. R., & Mouton, J. S. (1955). Status factors in pedestrain violation of traffic signals. *Journal of Abnormal Psychology* 51(3), 704–706.

## 23. What small change can have a BIG impact when it comes to positioning your team as experts?

More about the "cognitive response model" can be found in: Greenwald, A. G. (1968). Cognitive learning, cognitive response to persuasion, and attitude change. *Psychological Foundations of Attitudes* 147–170.

For the brain-imaging studies, see: Engelmann, J. B., Capra, C. M., Noussair, C., & Berns, G. S. (2009). Expert financial advice neurobiologically "offloads" financial decision-making under risk. *PLOS ONE* 4(3), e4957. doi:10.1371/journal.pone.0004957

The doctor introduction intervention is currently unpublished and part of the same Demand and Capacity experiment mentioned in chapter 5.

## 24. What unexpected small BIG can empower an uncertain expert?

The studies on (un)certain experts can be found in: Karmarkar, U. R., & Tormala, Z. L. (2010). Believe me, I have no idea what I'm talking about: The effects of source certainty on consumer involvement and persuasion. *Journal of Consumer Research* 36(6), 1033–1049.

### 25. What small BIG can prevent you from becoming the *Weakest Link*?

The *Weakest Link* and center-of-inattention research can be found in: Raghubir, P., & Valenzuela, A. (2006). Center-of-inattention: Position biases in decision-making. *Organizational Behavior and Human Decision Processes* 99(1), 66–80. doi:10.1016/j. obhdp.2005.06.001

For the chewing gum and related studies, see: Raghubir, P., & Valenzuela, A. (2009). Position based beliefs: The center stage effect. *Journal of Consumer Psychology* 19(2), 185–196.

### 26. What small BIG can encourage more creative thinking?

The plate size study can be found in Van Ittersum, K., & Wansink, B. (2012). Plate size and color suggestibility: The Delboeuf Illusion's bias on serving and eating behavior. *Journal of Consumer Research* 39(2), 215–228.

The tipping study can be found in: McCall, M., & Belmont, H. J. (1996). Credit card insignia and restaurant tipping: Evidence for an associative link. *Journal of Applied Psychology* 81(5), 609.

The voting study can be found in: Berger, J., Meredith, M., & Wheeler, S. C. (2008). Contextual priming: Where people vote affects how they vote. *Proceedings of the National Academy of Sciences* 105(26), 8846–8849.

The ceiling height study can be found in: Meyers-Levy, J., & Zhu, R. (2007). The influence of ceiling height: The effect of priming on the type of processing that people use. *Journal of Consumer Research* 34, 174–187.

### 27. How can a small change in venue lead to BIG differences in your negotiations?

For the home advantage study, see: Brown, G., & Baer, M. (2011). Location in negotiation: Is there a home field advantage?

*Organizational Behavior and Human Decision Processes* 114(2), 190–200. doi:10.1016/j.obhdp.2010.10.004

Courneya, K. S., & Carron, A. V. (1992). The home field advantage in sports competitions: A literature review. *Journal of Sport and Exercise Psychology* 14, 13–27.

## 28. What small BIG can improve both your power and your persuasiveness?

The warm drink equals warm heart study can be found in: Williams, L. E., & Bargh, J. A. (2008). Experiencing physical warmth promotes interpersonal warmth. *Science* 322(5901), 606–607.

You can find the power priming research in: Lammers, J., Dubois, D., Rucker, D. D., & Galinsky, A. D. (2013). Power gets the job: Priming power improves interview outcomes. *Journal of Experimental Social Psychology* 49(4), 776–779. doi:10.1016/j. jesp.2013.02.008

The study showing that adopting a high-power physical posture can increase feelings of power can be found in: Carney, D. R., Cuddy, A. J. C., & Yap, A. J. (2010). Power posing: Brief nonverbal displays cause changes in neuroendocrine levels and risk tolerance. *Psychological Science* 21, 1363–1368.

## 29. Why might love be the only small BIG you need?

The study conducted with pedestrians can be found in: Fischer-Lokou, J., Lamy, L., & Guéguen, N. (2009). Induced cognitions of love and helpfulness to lost persons. *Social Behavior and Personality* 37, 1213–1220.

For the "donating = loving" study, see: Guéguen, N., & Lamy, L. (2011). The effect of the word "love" on compliance to a request for humanitarian aid: An evaluation in a field setting. *Social Influence* 6(4), 249–58. doi:10.1080/15534510.2011.627771

The heart-shaped plate study can be found in: Guéguen, N. (2013). Helping with all your heart: The effect of cardioid dishes on tipping behavior. *Journal of Applied Social Psychology* 43(8), 1745–9. doi:10.1111/jasp.12109

### 30. What small BIG can help you find that perfect gift?

The gift studies can be found in: Gino, F., & Flynn, F. J. (2011). Give them what they want: The benefits of explicitness in gift exchange. *Journal of Experimental Social Psychology* 47(5), 915–22. doi:10.1016/j.jesp.2011.03.015

### 31. What BIG advantages can you gain when you take the small step of arranging to exchange?

For the favor-doing research, see: Flynn, F. J. (2003). How much should I give and how often? The effects of generosity and frequency of favor exchange on social status and productivity. *Academy of Management Journal* 46(5), 539–53. doi:10.2307/30040648

### 32. How could the small act of showing your appreciation make a BIG difference when influencing others?

The appreciation studies can be found in: Grant, A. M., & Gino, F. (2010). A little thanks goes a long way: Explaining why gratitude expressions motivate prosocial behavior. *Journal of Personality and Social Psychology* 98, 946–955.

### 33. Could unexpectedness be the small seed that reaps a BIG harvest?

For more on the British vicar and his "uncollection," see: http://www.bbc.co.uk/news/uk-22012215.

The restaurant-tipping study can be found in: Strohmetz, D. B., Rind, B., Fisher, R., & Lynn, M. (2002). Sweetening the till: The use of candy to increase restaurant tipping. *Journal of Applied Social Psychology* 32(2), 300–309.

The study showing how consumers react more favorably to
unexpected coupons can be found in: Heilman, C. M.,
Nakamoto, K., & Rao, A. G. (2002). Pleasant surprises:
Consumer response to unexpected in-store coupons. *Journal of
Marketing Research*, 242–252.

## 34. What surprisingly simple small BIG can get you the help you need?

For the studies on asking for help, see: Flynn, F. J., & Lake, V. K. B.
(2008). If you need help, just ask: Underestimating compliance
with direct requests for help. *Journal of Personality and Social
Psychology* 95(1), 128–143. doi:10.1037/0022-3514.95.1.128

The research showing that helpers tend to overestimate the
likelihood that a requester will ask for help can be found in:
Bohns, V. K., & Flynn, F. J. (2010). "Why didn't you just ask?"
Underestimating the discomfort of help-seeking. *Journal of
Experimental Social Psychology* 46(2), 402–409.

## 35. What small BIG can make the difference when it comes to effective negotiation?

The research on making the first offer in negotiations can be
found in: Galinsky, A., & Mussweiler, T. (2001). First offers as
anchors: The role of perspective-taking and negotiator focus.
*Journal of Personality and Social Psychology* 81(4), 657–669.
doi:10.1037//0022-3514.81.4.657

## 36. Could precision be the small BIG when it comes to better bargaining?

For the studies on precise offers, see: Mason, M. F., Lee, A. J., Wiley,
E, A., & Ames, D. R. (2013). Precise offers are potent anchors:
Conciliatory counteroffers and attributions of knowledge in
negotiations. *Journal of Experimental Social Psychology* 49(4),
759–763. doi:10.1016/j.jesp.2013.02.012

### 37. Why might a small change in number ending make a BIG difference to your communications?

A nice review of the origins of odd and 99-cent price endings can be found in: Gendall, P., Holdershaw, J., & Garland, R. (1997). The effect of odd pricing on demand. *European Journal of Marketing* 31(11/12), 799–813.

For the research on .99 price endings, see: Gaston-Breton, C., & Duque, L. (2012). Promotional benefits of 99-ending prices: The moderating role of intuitive and analytical decision style. In *Proceedings of the 41st Conference of the European Marketing Academy (EMAC)*. Lisbon, Portugal.

More information about the levelling-down effect can be found in: Stirving, M., & Winer, R. (1997). An empirical analysis of price ending with scanner data. *Journal of Consumer Research* 24, 57–67.

The pen study can be found in: Manning, K. C., & Sprott, D. E. (2009). Price endings, left-digit effects, and choice. *Journal of Consumer Research* 36(2), 328–335. doi:10.1086/597215

### 38. Could a small change in order be the BIG difference that wins you more orders?

For the item-price order study, see: Bagchi, R., & Davis, D. F. (2012). $29 for 70 items or 70 items for $29? How presentation order affects package perceptions. *Journal of Consumer Research* 39(1), 62–73. doi:10.1086/661893

### 39. What small BIG could end up getting you a lot more for much less?

The additive versus averaging effect studies can be found in: Weaver, K., Garcia, S. M., & Schwarz, N. (2012). The presenter's paradox. *Journal of Consumer Research* 39(3), 445–460. doi:10.1086/664497

For the research on the "and that's not all" approach, see: Burger, J. M. (1986). Increasing compliance by improving the deal: The that's-not-all technique. *Journal of Personality and Social Psychology* 51(2), 277–283. doi:10.1037//0022–3514.51.2.277

## 40. How could the small act of unit-asking make a BIG difference to your appeals?

For the donation study, see: Hsee, C. K., Zhang, J., Lu, Z. Y., & Xu, F. (2013). Unit asking: A method to boost donations and beyond. *Psychological Science* 24(9), 1801–1808. doi:10.1177/0956797613482947

## 41. Why would highlighting identifiable features be the small BIG that boosts your campaign efforts?

For more on the impact of attaching a photograph to a CT scan, see: Wendling, P. (2009). Can a photo enhance a radiologist's report? *Clinical Endocrinology News* 4(2), 6.

A nice report on the same can be found at http://www.nytimes.com/2009/04/07/health/07pati.html.

For more on the "identifiable victim" effect in donations, see: Small, D. A., & Loewenstein, G. (2003). Helping the victim or helping a victim: Altruism and identifiability. *Journal of Risk and Uncertainty* 26(1), 5–16.

For the "identifiable victim" effect in medical decisions, see: Redelmeier, D. A., & Tversky, A. (1990). Discrepancy between medical decisions for individual patients and for groups. *The New England Journal of Medicine* 322, 1162–1164.

The "identified intervention" effect studies can be found in: Cryder, C. E., Loewenstein, G., & Scheines, R. (2013). The donor is in the details. *Organizational Behavior and Human Decision Processes* 120(1), 15–23. doi:10.1016/j.obhdp.2012.08.002

## 42. What small BIG can ensure that your costs are not opportunities lost?

For the studies on opportunity cost neglect, see: Frederick, S., Novemsky, N., Wang, J., Dhar, R., & Nowlis, S. (2009). Opportunity cost neglect. *Journal of Consumer Research* 36(4), 553–561. doi:10.1086/599764

## 43. What small BIG can help to motivate others (and yourself) to complete tasks?

The loyalty program study can be found in: Koo, M., & Fishbach, A. (2012). The small-area hypothesis: Effects of progress monitoring on goal adherence. *Journal of Consumer Research* 39(3), 493–509. doi:10.1086/663827

## 44. What small BIG can lead to greater customer loyalty?

The yogurt study can be found in: Jin, L., Huang, S., & Zhang, Y. (in press). The unexpected positive impact of fixed structures on goal completion. *Journal of Consumer Research.*

## 45. How could a small BIG result in 1 + 1 getting you more than 2?

The research on dividing rewards into categories can be found in: Wiltermuth, S., & Gino, F. (2013). "I'll have one of each": How separating rewards into (meaningless) categories increases motivation. *Journal of Personality and Social Psychology* 104(1), 1–13.

The paper that discusses the often detrimental tendency to pay off small rather than larger debts first can be found in: Amar, M., Ariely, D., Ayal, S., Cryder, C., & Rick, S. (2011). Winning the battle but losing the war: The psychology of debt management. *Journal of Marketing Research* 48 (SPL), S38–S50.

## 46. How could a small step back lead to a BIG leap forward?

For the studies on the influence of physical distance, see: Thomas, M., & Tsai, C. I. (2012). Psychological distance and subjective experience: How distancing reduces the feeling of difficulty. *Journal of Consumer Research* 39(2), 324–340. doi:10.1086/663772

## 47. How can you make BIG strides from others' small stumbles?

For the review of research on negative information, see: Baumeister, R. F., Bratslavsky, E., Finkenauer, C., & Vohs, K. D. (2001). Bad is stronger than good. *Review of General Psychology* 5(4), 323–370. doi:10.1037//1089–2680.5.4.323

## 48. How could a small shift from error banishment to error management lead to BIG success?

For more on lifespan research, see: Seery, M. D., Holman, E. A., & Silver, R. C. (2010). Whatever does not kill us: Cumulative lifetime adversity, vulnerability, and resilience. *Journal of Personality and Social Psychology* 99, 1025–1041.

You can find the research on error management training in: Keith, N., & Frese, M. (2008). Effectiveness of error management training: A meta-analysis. *Journal of Applied Psychology* 93, 59–69.

You can find the customer experience article in: Schrange, M. (2004, September). The opposite of perfect: Why solving problems rather than preventing them can better satisfy your customers. *Sales & Marketing Management* 26.

**49.** How could a small change in timing make a BIG difference to your online reviews?

The impact of the timing of a review on word of mouth can be found in: Chen, Z., & Lurie, N. (2013). Temporal contiguity and negativity bias in the impact of online word-of-mouth. *Journal of Marketing Research* 50(4), 463–476

**50.** What small change can you make to an email that can make a BIG difference to how easy your business partners are to negotiate with?

You can find the two humor studies in: Kurtzberg, T. R., Naquin, C. E., & Belkin, L. Y. (2009). Humor as a relationship-building tool in online negotiations. *International Journal of Conflict Management* 20(4), 377–397. doi:10.1108/10444060910991075

The study that examined the effect of disclosing personal information before a negotiation can be found in: Moore, D., Kurtzberg, T., Thompson, L., & Morris, M. (1999). Long and short routes to success in electronically mediated negotiations: Group affiliations and good vibrations. *Organizational Behavior and Human Decision Processes* 77(1), 22–43. doi:10.1006/obhd.1998.2814

The pet frog joke study can be found in: O'Quinn, K., & Aronoff, J. (1981). Humor as a technique of social influence. *Social Psychology Quarterly* 44(4), 349–357.

**51.** How might a small touch lead to a BIG increase in value?

The research on touch can be found in: Peck, J., & Shu, S. B. (2009). The effect of mere touch on perceived ownership. *Journal of Consumer Research* 36(3), 434–447. doi:10.1086/598614

## 52. Saving the best 'til last. What small BIG can make all the difference?

For the colonoscopy study, see: Redelmeier, D., Katz, J., & Kahneman, D. (2003). Memories of colonoscopy: A randomized trial. *Pain* 104(1–2), 187–194.

## The small BIG: Bonus Chapter

For the health center no-show study, see Martin, S. J., Bassi, S., & Dunbar-Rees, R. (2012). Commitments, norms and custard creams—a social influence approach to reducing did not attends (DNAs). *Journal of the Royal Society of Medicine* 105(3),101–104.

The study combining social norms and incentives can be found in: Dolan, P., & Metcalfe, R. (2013). *Neighbors, Knowledge, and Nuggets: Two Natural Field Experiments on the Role of Incentives on Energy Conservation* (CEP discussion paper no. 1222). Centre for Economic Performance, London School of Economics.

More information regarding the three fundamental motives discussed can be found in: Cialdini, R. B., & Goldstein, N. J. (2004). Social influence: Compliance and conformity. *Annual Review of Psychology*, 55, 591–621.

More details of the experiments combining egoistic and altruistic appeals can be found in: Feiler, D. C., Tost, L. P., & Grant, A. M. (2012). Mixed reasons, missed givings: The costs of blending egoistic and altruistic reasons in donation requests. *Journal of Experimental Social Psychology* 48(6), 1322–1328.

The work showing three to be the optimal number of appeals can be found in Shu, S. B., & Carlson, K. A. (2014). When three charms but four alarms: Identifying the optimal number of claims in persuasion settings. *Journal of Marketing* 78(1), 127–139.

# Index

Printed in Great Britain
by Amazon